Japanese Political Economy Revisited

During the last 30 years, the Japanese political economy system has experienced significant changes that are usually not well understood or analysed because of their complexity and contradictions. This book provides new analyses and insights on the process of evolving Japanese political economy including Japan's current economic policy known as Abenomics. The first three chapters looks at evolutions at the corporate level, characterised in recent years by increasing firm heterogeneity. The authors apply theoretically driven analyses to the complex subject of corporate governance, human resource management and corporate reporting by discussing new developments in context of their economic opportunities as well as of their institutional contradictions with continuities in Japanese business practices. The second group of chapters deals with institutional changes and evolving economic reforms on the macro level of political economy. The two chapters focus on the financial system regulation and economic growth policies as two central elements of Japan's political economy and key drivers in the evolution of its economy. Their analysis allows us to better understand the interplay between reforms and change in consumption credit and to reinterpret Abenomics as a manifestation of ongoing contradictions within the Japanese political economy.

The chapters in this book were originally published as a special issue of *Japan Forum.*

David Chiavacci is Professor in Social Science of Japan at the University of Zurich, Switzerland. His recent publications include *Social Movements and Political Activism in Contemporary Japan* (Routledge 2018, co-edited with Julia Obinger) and *Social Inequality in Post-growth Japan* (Routledge 2017, co-edited with Carola Hommerich).

Sébastien Lechevalier is Professor at the École des Hautes Études en Sciences Sociale, (Paris, France) and President of Fondation France Japon (http://ffj.ehess.fr/). His research interests lie from Asian capitalisms to issues related to the role of the state in development and welfare. His recent publications includes *The great transformation of Japanese capitalism* (Routledge, 2014) and *Innovation beyond technology: Science for society and interdisciplinary approaches* (2018, co-edited with Yuko Fujigaki and Sandra Laugier).

Japanese Political Economy Revisited

Abenomics and Institutional Change

Edited by
David Chiavacci and Sébastien Lechevalier

Routledge
Taylor & Francis Group
LONDON AND NEW YORK

First published 2019
by Routledge

2 Park Square, Milton Park, Abingdon, Oxfordshire OX14 4RN
52 Vanderbilt AVenue, New York, NY 10017

Routledge is an imprint of the Taylor & Francis Group, an informa business

First issued in paperback 2020

British Library Cataloguing in Publication Data
A catalogue record for this book is available from the British Library

ISBN 13: 978-1-138-60694-4 (hbk)
ISBN 13: 978-0-367-66156-4 (pbk)

Typeset in Plantin
by RefineCatch Limited, Bungay, Suffolk

Publisher's Note
The publisher accepts responsibility for any inconsistencies that may have arisen during the conversion of this book from journal articles to book chapters, namely the possible inclusion of journal terminology.

Contents

Citation Information

The chapters in this book were originally published in *Japan Forum*, volume 29, issue 3 (September 2017). When citing this material, please use the original page numbering for each article, as follows:

Chapter 1
Japanese political economy revisited: diverse corporate change, institutional transformation, and Abenomics
David Chiavacci and Sébastian Lechevalier
Japan Forum, volume 29, issue 3 (September 2017), pp. 299–311

Chapter 2
Change and continuity in Japanese corporate reform
Mitsuharu Miyamoto
Japan Forum, volume 29, issue 3 (September 2017), pp. 312–337

Chapter 3
Shareholding characteristics and imperfect coverage of the Stewardship Code in Japan
Ryohei Nakagawa
Japan Forum, volume 29, issue 3 (September 2017), pp. 338–353

Chapter 4
'Growth oriented' corporate governance reform – can it solve Japan's performance puzzle?
Franz Waldenberger
Japan Forum, volume 29, issue 3 (September 2017), pp. 354–374

Chapter 5
The Japanese consumer finance market and its institutional changes since the 1980s
Adrienne Sala
Japan Forum, volume 29, issue 3 (September 2017), pp. 375–398

Chapter 6

Re-packaging old policies? 'Abenomics' and the lack of an alternative growth model for Japan's political economy
Saori Shibata
Japan Forum, volume 29, issue 3 (September 2017), pp. 399–422

Notes on Contributors

David Chiavacci is Professor in Social Science of Japan at University of Zurich, Institute of Asian and Oriental Studies, Switzerland.

Sébastien Lechevalier is Professor at the École des Hautes Études en Sciences Sociale (Paris, France) and President of Fondation France Japon (http://ffj.ehess.fr/).

Mitsuharu Miyamoto is Professor at Senshu University, School of Economics, Tokyo, Japan.

Ryohei Nakagawa is Associate Professor at Kyoto University of Foreign Studies, Japan.

Adrienne Sala is Postdoctoral Researcher at University Paris 7 Paris Diderot, France.

Saori Shibata is Lecturer at Leiden University, Leiden Institute for Area Studies, The Netherlands.

Franz Waldenberger is Director of the German Institute for Japanese Studies, Tokyo, Japan.

Japanese political economy revisited: diverse corporate change, institutional transformation, and Abenomics

DAVID CHIAVACCI AND SÉBASTIEN LECHEVALIER

Abstract: This introductory article to the special issue on "Japanese Political Economy Revisited: Diverse Corporate Change, Institutional Transformation, and Abenomics" starts with a short summaryof the changing perceptions of Japan's political economy from its meteoric rise as worldwide leading model in the 1970s and 1980s to its demotiontoa problem and reform case since the later 1990s. Based on this overview, it identifies some striking issue and open questions in this conventional view of Japan's political economy as problem and the high expectations on Abenomics as Japan's current economic reform programme. Then we discuss the articles of the special issue and their new contributionsto a better understanding of the developments at the corporate level as well as institutional change and economic reforms at the macro level in the last two decades. Finally, this introductory article ends with a short outlineof a new research programme and four central research questions about the Japanese political economy.

The Japanese political economy, beyond conventional wisdom

Over the last 30 years, the Japanese political economy system has experienced significant changes that are usually not well understood or well analysed, given their complexity and contradictions. After a decline of interest in the Japanese economy, it is possible to detect a revival, which utilises the tools of institutional analysis applied to Asian capitalism (Boyer *et al.* 2011, Storz *et al.* 2013). The strong mass media attention, but also academic interest in Abenomics, has further reinforced this new research interest on institutional change in Japan's economy. The purpose of the collection of articles included in this special issue is to provide new insights into the process of the evolving Japanese political economy.

As the Japanese economy has experienced two decades of economic stagnation, apparently similar to the one experienced by most European countries, one often forgets the epistemological shock that it produced in the 1970s and the 1980s (Dore 1973, Ouchi 1981, Pascale and Athos 1981, Johnson 1982, Altshuler *et al.* 1984, Womack *et al.* 1990, Lazonick 1991), when it overcame all the European economies and seemed to be on the way to becoming the number one economy in the world. The origin of interest for the Japanese economy in the 1970s and the 1980s indeed comes from the differentiated performance of the Japanese economy on the one side and of the US and European economies on the other side, both in terms of growth and trade. This performance of the Japanese economy was all the more disturbing since a simple economic analysis shows that the way it was functioning at the micro and macro levels was far from the laws of market economy as taught in economics textbooks. For example, Japanese firms certainly maximised their profits, as American or European firms did, but some of their decisions – such as keeping non-profitable activities or avoiding lay-offs in case of negative shocks – show that profit was only one variable among others (such as growth, which is the condition of long-term employment) in the objectives' function. Stated differently, not only did Japanese capitalism not seem to follow the basic rules of a market economy, it seemed to be more efficient.

Moreover, Japan seemed to Western observers to represent an alternative modernity that might be worth emulating by the US and European societies (Kahn 1970, Vogel 1979, Sugimoto 2014, pp. 24–28). Comparative research showed that it achieved a high degree of socio-economic equality without extensive redistribution through a comprehensive welfare state and high taxes, as in the Scandinavian countries. Japan was a prime example for a productivist welfare regime, in which welfare programmes and benefits were small in international comparison. Instead, state policies implemented functional equivalents that guaranteed social integration and cohesion. Although state expenditures for the education system were much lower than the OECD average, its students made it to the very top in comparative international surveys on education level. Its school system was described as highly meritocratic, which made Japan not only an equal, but also a fair society. Regarding industrial relations, Japan was known for its close cooperation between management and unions at the company level as a foundation for the highly efficient production system of Japanese companies.

This period is now over. Japan is no longer a role model from which to learn, but a problem case to be solved. Hence, academic research has concentrated on the long stagnation of the Japanese economy. More policy oriented or normative studies have proposed some solutions based on structural reform discourses very similar to the one applied everywhere in the world since the mid-1980s (Lincoln 2001, Mulgan 2002, Ito *et al.* 2005, Pesek 2014). It is possible to summarise as follows the dominant vision about the Japanese economy from the early 1990s:

the fact that the Japanese system has not adapted itself well to a new environment explains the poor performance of the Japanese economy since the early 1990s. More precisely, the simple discourse is that the 'decay' of Japan (whose symbol would be demography) can be explained by the absence of reforms in a new environment characterised by new phases of globalisation and technical progress, rendering a radical reform of the former model necessary. This type of discourse is in fact very similar to the one in Europe that analyses the so-called *eurosclerosis*.

This vision of the Japanese economy is very popular and is very rarely criticised. It is not only dominant among foreign pundits and researchers, but also highly influential inside Japan in public discussions and among policy-making circles. This vision also explains why some foreign observers and many in Japan received Abenomics so positively and had such high expectations for it. A contribution of this special issue is to show the limitations of this vision, in underlining the poor job it does in explaining a series of striking issues.

A series of striking issues and open questions

First of all, the conventional wisdom about the Japanese political economy underestimates the extent and intensity of changes the economy has experienced at both the micro and institutional level. Moreover, it does not explain why these changes, whose major aim was to promote a convergence towards to the – partly fantasised – US type of liberal capitalist economy, did not lead to such a transformation and convergence of this ideal type. Moreover, at the firm level, we observe an increasing diversity in terms of organisation and performance, which is not explained (Lechevalier 2014). Second, although the aim of the series of structural reforms introduced since the mid-1980s was to improve the efficiency of the Japanese economy, rather the contrary has been observed (Boyer *et al.* 2011).

Third, conventional wisdom does not adequately take into consideration the social embeddedness of Japan's political economy. Its success up to the 1990s and its crisis since the 1990s are connected to what we might call the 'Japanese way of life' as a social contract between Japan's elites and population (Chiavacci 2007). In this ideal life course, stability and security are priorities, and it is expected that high educational attainments will be translated into stable employment and internal careers in the cooperative and protective community of the employer. It was also connected to strongly differentiated gender roles with men ideally taking up the role as main breadwinner and lifetime employed salaryman (*salarīman*) and women concentrating on being education mothers (*kyōiku mama*) in their role as centre of the family and especially the educational success of the children. Up to the mid-1990s, an increasing majority of the population was highly optimistic of accomplishing (at least partially) this ideal life course model and, hence, to be fully integrated into Japan's success story, in which educational investment and the hard work of men and women was compensated through secure employment, income and a continuation of this success story in the next generation. Since the proclamation of Ikeda's double income plan in 1960, the Liberal Democratic Party (LDP) was not only the guarantor of economic growth, but also that the fruits of this growth would be fairly distributed through the Japanese way of life among the whole population. While foreign observers might have seen Japan primarily as a champion of economic growth, from a Japanese perspective the main point was that Japan was a prime example of shared growth. The Japanese way of life was attractive. From the 1970s onwards, it even evolved into a prescriptive model, not only promising a better and brighter life, but also stipulating how to live one's life and how to educate one's children. Since the 1990s, structural change and diversification, like the de-standardisation of employment and increasing differences among firms, even of the same size and in the same sector, has not totally disrupted this life course model, but has significantly eroded it. It has led to a new insecurity and a feeling of crisis that has reached even those in Japan's core middle classes that have not yet been directly affected by these changes. While formerly a large majority firmly believed in the opportunity of fully participating in Japan's shared growth, now the society is marked by increasing inequalities and its division into winners and losers. And nobody seems to be immune from the risk of be sucked into the loser group. This has led to high levels of social anxiety and societal pessimism in current Japan (Yamada 2004, Allison 2013, Kakei Keizai Kenkyūjo 2015, Tanabiki and Miyata 2015, Hommerich 2016, van Houwelingen 2016). Conventional wisdom, hence, ignores the crumbling social foundation of Japan's political economy. Its recommendations might even be counterproductive, as liberal reforms will most likely further increase feelings of insecurity among the population.

A concrete example of the limitations of conventional wisdom is the interpretation of the Japanese 'crisis'. Although the purpose of this special issue is not an analysis of the crisis in Japan from the early 1990s but rather a study of institutional change, this issue proposes an original interpretation of the Japanese crisis, based on the analysis of the implications of the rise of corporate diversity. In doing this, we disagree with explanations that see in the stagnation the results of a series of short-term policy mistakes (e.g. Mikitani and Posen 2000). They certainly played a role but cannot account for the duration of this stagnation, which should be explained by some structural factors. Our analysis is an institutionalist one that criticises dominant institutionalist interpretations of the Japanese crisis, those, among others, that emphasise the lack of organisational diversity at the micro level (Aoki 2000) or which see in the over-coordination of Japanese capitalism the source of the lack of social change (Witt 2006). As for the first thesis, we provide a clear contradiction with stylised facts in this special issue, focusing on increasing corporate diversity.

In this context, the Japanese crisis – its intensity and its duration – cannot be explained by the absence of institutional change but rather by disruptions in the former system and the emergence of structural incompatibilities, which come from a lack of coherence and coordination. If this analysis of the Japanese crisis is correct, the revival of the Japanese economy lies in its re-coordination. We do not deny the importance of short-term economic policies, as the European case presently shows, through the inability of the European Commission and national governments to define an articulated growth strategy that is not restricted to austerity measures or does not start with them. However, coherence and coordination are the alpha and the omega of growth, as the case of Abenomics shows.

From a perspective of economic sociology, one exemplary aspect to identify these disruptions in the former system and the emergence of structural incompatibilities is the relation between the growth model and questions of inequality. In the former system, shared growth was the foundation of an equal Japan and, hence, the high degree of social integration in a large part of the population. Although some research questions the dominant perspective of post war Japan up to the mid-1990s having a highly equal income distribution per household and a highly meritocratic school system that led to a structural openness for social mobility (Ishizaki 1983, Ishida 1993), the high growth led to a very high level of absolute social upward mobility and generally increasing purchasing power. This general upgrading of the Japanese society overrode in everyday life the question of distribution and led to shared growth experienced by a large majority of the population. As shared growth is no longer taken for granted, questions of inequality have gained a completely new meaning (Chiavacci 2008, Chiavacci and Hommerich 2016). In recent decades, household incomes are decreasing or stagnating (even during periods of continuous growth of about 2 per cent from 2003 to 2007), careers are focusing on restructuring and increasing atypical employment, which is becoming more and more insecure, and even a university degree can no longer be taken as a guarantee for socio-economic stability. In view of this social crisis, much more than just some structural reforms and a new money policy are needed in order to bring Japan back on track. The small welfare state had a long-time advantage for Japan, but in view of the end of shared growth and secure employment as its main functional equivalents, a fundamental rethinking of Japan's productivistic welfare regime seems unavoidable.

Major findings and implications of the special issue

This special issue includes five articles that we believe are all important contributions to the understanding of the contemporary Japanese political economy, especially from the viewpoint of the issues we have underlined previously. The major originality of this special issue lies in the coherence and quality of the set of articles it includes. Despite their diversity in terms of theory and methodology, each article is a theoretically well-founded analysis and develops a new contribution to recent approaches on corporate and institutional changes as well as economic reforms in Japan (Hoshi and Kashyap 2001, Amyx 2004, Jacoby 2005, Olcott 2005, Sako 2006, Vogel 2006, Aoki *et al.* 2007, Tiberghien 2007, Cargill and Sakamoto 2008, Whittaker and Deakin 2009, Park and Patrick 2013, Lechevalier 2014).

The first group of three articles, by Mitsuharu Miyamoto, Ryohei Nakagawa and Franz Waldenberger, looks at evolutions at the corporate level, characterised in recent years by increasing firm heterogeneity in both organisations and performance that concerns various fields including corporate governance and employment practices. The perspective primarily comes from management studies and historical political economy. While corporate governance reform efforts as part of Abenomics have been lauded in leading Western mass media publications as a 'revolution in the making' that will lead to new growth and wealth in Japan (*The Economist* 2014, 2015, de Swaan 2015), the three authors apply a much more subtle and theoretically driven analysis to the complex subject of corporate governance, human resource management and corporate reporting by discussing new developments in the context of their economic opportunities as well as in the context of their institutional contradictions with continuities in Japanese business practices.

The first contribution, by Miyamoto, analyses the relationship between reforms in corporate governance in Japanese companies and their human resource management. His main finding is an increasing diversity among Japanese companies concerning corporate governance as well as human resource management. While only a few Japanese companies have shifted completely to a shareholder-oriented corporate governance, à la the US, many companies have de facto introduced incremental changes in their corporate governance. Miyamoto shows in his analysis that this cumulative change in board structures also resulted in adaptation in human resource management in Japanese companies, which restricted life-time employment and introduced performance-related pay. However, these developments are not homogenously evolving in the same direction and by the same degree in Japanese companies, but show large variance, which allows for identifying different types of companies that have emerged in recent decades.

Waldenberger's article addresses whether the envisaged corporate governance reform as a central element of Abenomics will really lead to higher productivity and growth in Japan. The reasoning for a positive answer to this question is that underperformance of Japan's economy cannot be attributed to missing efforts in research and development or a qualitatively poor workforce and missing financial capital, but is the result of risk avoidance of boards because they include no company outsiders. However, Waldenberger shows that the argument for a direct impact of a company's board composition on its performance is not persuasive. Both factors are, in fact, in his view influenced by a third factor, which leads to this spurious correlation. This third factor is the dominance of in-house careers among board members. Accordingly, Waldenberger argues that the current governance reforms will not by themselves solve the underperformance problem of the Japanese economy. Still, he regards them as a possible stimulus for new forms of human resource management that may lead in the long term to higher productivity and more growth.

Finally, Nakagawa's contribution in this first group of articles discusses the potential impact of the Japanese Stewardship Code, which was introduced in 2014, on the engagement of shareholders in corporate governance. He differentiates between institutional investors as outsiders versus mutual cross shareholdings between companies or companies and banks as insiders. The proportion of outsiders among the shareholders has significantly increased since the late 1990s. In fact, since the early 2000s, they have overtaken insiders as shareholders. Overall, this transition has not only led to much shorter investment periods, but also corporate management has shortened its time horizon. While insiders still tend to hold stocks longer, they seldom actively engage in the corporate governance in their role as investors. According to Nakagawa's analysis, the new Stewardship Code will only have a limited impact and will not trigger stable market growth as intended. While the Code demands investors actively engage in corporate governance, it is only directed at outsiders. By not covering insiders as a significant and potentially important investors group, the effect will be limited.

Overall, these three articles show not only the increasing heterogeneity among, but also new internal contradictions in, Japanese companies in their investor relations, corporate governance and human resource management. Well-intended reforms and new developments on the corporate level have often happened on an ad hoc basis with no comprehensive plan and in reaction to external pressures and new ideas. This has weakened and often even undermined the institutional complementarities between investor relations, corporate governance and human resource management. In the larger societal picture, this reduction in institutional complementarities is an important factor that has contributed to rising insecurity and constant questioning of the future of the Japanese way of life. Recent and envisaged reforms as part of Abenomics have been lauded as important measures to lead Japanese companies back to a path of growth and higher productivity, but the analysis in the group of articles shows that these reforms have limitations and, at best, only a partial impact. Hence, it remains highly questionable if they can solve the internal fragmentation, in addition they might actually further enhance the internal fragmentation and its negative societal impact.

The second group of articles, by Adrienne Sala and Saori Shibata, deals with institutional change and evolving economic reforms at the macro level of Japan's political economy. The articles focus on the financial system regulation and economic growth policies as central elements of Japan's political economy and key drivers in the evolution of its economy. Rather than adopting the usual short-term view, the articles adopt a political economy perspective that allows for connecting economic policies and reforms to overall institutional and social change. From this viewpoint, it is possible to better understand the interplay between reforms and change in consumption credit and to reinterpret Abenomics not as an accident but rather as a manifestation of ongoing contradictions within the Japanese political economy.

The article by Shibata is a comprehensive and innovative analysis of Abenomics. Her analysis highlights the internal contradictions in Abenomics between its first two arrows, which are Keynesian-styled remedies, and the third arrow, which encompasses a wide range of liberal-oriented structural reforms that have been preached for decades to Japan as part of the conventional wisdom identified above. Shibata regards these two strategies as mutually incompatible and, hence, assesses Abenomics not as a set of really new reform policies leading to an alternative growth model of Japan in the long-term, but as a re-packaging of older policies by former administrations that, due to their internal contradictions, pose a risk to the long-term stability of Japan's capitalism. As a main problem, she identifies the stagnating wages that lead to a weak demand. This is not only unsolved by Abenomics, but the envisaged deregulation of the labour market might even contribute to a further increase in wage insecurity and social instability.

Sala analyses, in the second contribution on the macro-level, the institutional change in the Japanese consumer finance market since the 1980s. During the economic downturn and stagnation from the 1990s onwards, the weakly regulated and unsecure personal loan market led to an increase in indebtedness and over-borrowing among the lower income households and resulted in a stark increase in bankruptcies in Japan. The market share of consumer finance companies, which use illicit and harsh practices, strongly increased in those years. The rising salience and increasing press coverage of these issues forced the Japanese government to enact reforms and a stronger regulation of the consumer finance market from 2006 to 2010. Sala points out that public debates and political reforms did not address the causes of rising social inequality that led to over-borrowing and rising bankruptcies, but that the reforms show the rising influence of civil society actors in policy making, which resulted in better consumer protection.

Overall, the analyses on the macro-level show darker and brighter developments. Although Abenomics is already lauded by some as a success story (*The Economist* 2016), as Shibata points out, it does not address the central malaise of Japan's capitalism. Without reinforced security of one's social integration, overcoming decreasing purchasing power and stronger demand, the Japanese economy will not return to a path of shared growth and actually to any long-term growth at all. In fairness, it has to be pointed out that Abe and his advisory team are not totally unaware of this main problem, which is also key for finally escaping deflation and provoking significant inflation in Japan (Everaert and Ganelli 2016, Lechevalier and Monfort 2016, Porcellacchia 2016). Since 2012, Abe and his cabinet have repeatedly been campaigning for pay increases for all workers including those of small and medium-size companies (SME). For a conservative, business-friendly Prime Minister and administration, this an unexpected form of conduct, which has been nicknamed the 'governmental spring offensive' (*kansei shuntō*) by Japan's mass media (*Mainichi Shinbun* 2015a, 2016, Murata 2015). With the same aims, the current government has also decided to increase the minimum wage by an average of 18 Yen to a national average of 798 Yen, which is the highest hike since 2002 (*Mainichi Shinbun* 2015b). However, the results of this governmental pay offensive have been negligible. National statistics show still stagnating incomes in recent years (MIAC 2016, p. 138). According to a representative survey in February 2015, only 13 per cent of the respondents personally experienced a positive economic effect of Abenomics (*Nihon Keizai Shinbun* 2015). The urgency felt by the government to reassure the population and re-establish shared growth is obvious in the revised version of Abenomics presented in September 2015 (Prime Minister of Japan and His Cabinet 2015). With this kind of Abenomics 2.0, three new arrows were announced: (1) 'robust economic growth that gives rise to hope', (2) 'dream-weaving childcare support', and (3) 'social security that provides reassurance'. While the first new arrow aims at an enhancement and combination of the prior three arrows of the first version of Abenomics, the second and third are directed solely at the domestic audience, moving beyond economic policies into social welfare. Still, to what degree this social policy reform agenda will be realised remains to be seen. In this context, Sala's analysis may also offer some hope. Her article shows that through the involvement of civil society and increasing public pressure, more balanced reforms for consumers and producers as well as employers and employees are not impossible. However, it must also be noted that the crisis of Japan's capitalism and social contract has led to some new forms of political mobilisation and contestation, but 'the impact of such contestation on policymaking and actual policies has thus far been limited' (Shibata 2016, p. 496). In fact, the temporary deselection of the LDP from political power was primarily the result of established vested interests in rural Japan and not of new social movements or civil society actors (Chiavacci 2010). The voice of the people is, however, needed in order to find a lasting new foundation and social contract for Japan. It has to be remembered that the former social contract of shared growth and its Japanese way of life was the result of fierce and open socio-economic conflicts in the early post-war decades.

Towards a new research programme for the Japanese political economy

We hope that this special issue on Japan's political economy and corporate governance will not only be of interest for Japanese studies, but will also stimulate more interdisciplinary research on Japan's political economy and capitalism. In recent years, besides a few exceptions such as Pempel and Muramatsu (2014), the economy and political economy as topics have been generally absent from Japanese studies journals such as *Japan Forum*.

The major aim of this special issue is not only to contribute to the debates between economists but to open these debates up to scholars from different disciplines. We are indeed convinced that the 'closure' of economics and political economy to other disciplines is detrimental to the understanding of some key issues of contemporary Japan, whose complexity requires multidisciplinary approaches. Japan's economic stagnation is, on the one hand, undermining the former social contract between Japan's elites and population. On the other hand, this unaddressed societal crisis has also led to the prolongation of the economic standstill. In other words, Japan's economy and capitalism are too important to leave to the standard economists.

Among the questions that have to be addressed by reference to the Japanese context and in international comparison, let us mention four:

- How can we conceptualise the revival of the intervention of the State in a context characterised by maturity (post-development) and liberalisation?
- Whereas social protection essentially relied on family and firms, how do we understand the rise of a social state in Asia, without any subordination to a productivist logic, as in the former model?
- How can the liberalisation of markets explain the increasing diversity of firms, in terms of organisation and performance?
- What would a new social contract look like as a new foundation for Japan's capitalism and society?

Despite their diversity, these questions converge towards the idea that a renewal of our approach to the Japanese political economy is necessary: it should be more comparative and more interdisciplinary. If this special issue can arouse, in this direction, a new wave of research on institutional change in Japan, then one of its goals will have been achieved.

Disclosure statement

No potential conflict of interest was reported by the authors.

References

Allison, A., 2013. *Precarious Japan*. Durham: Duke University Press.

Altshuler, A., *et al.*, 1984. *The future of the automobile: the report of MIT's international automobile program*. Cambridge: MIT Press.

Amyx, J.A., 2004. *Japan's financial crisis: institutional rigidity and reluctant change*. Princeton: Princeton University Press.

Aoki, M., 2000. *Information, corporate governance, and institutional diversity: competitiveness in Japan, the USA, and the transitional economies*. Oxford: Oxford University Press.

Aoki, M., Jackson, G., and Miyajima, H., eds., 2007. *Corporate governance in Japan: institutional change and organizational diversity*. Oxford: Oxford University Press.

Boyer, R., Uemura, H., and Isogai, A., eds., 2011. *Diversity and transformations of Asian capitalisms*. London: Routledge.

Cargill, T.F. and Sakamoto, T., 2008. *Japan since 1980*. Cambridge: Cambridge University Press.

Chiavacci, D., 2007. The social basis of developmental capitalism in Japan: from postwar mobilization to current stress symptoms and future disintegration. *Asian Business & Management*, 6 (1), 35–55.

Chiavacci, D., 2008. From class struggle to general middle-class society to divided society: societal models of inequality in Postwar Japan. *Social Science Japan Journal*, 11 (1), 5–27.

Chiavacci, D., 2010. Divided society model and social cleavages in Japanese politics: no alignment by social class, but dealignment of rural-urban split. *Contemporary Japan*, 22 (1/2), 47–74.

Chiavacci, D. and Hommerich, C., eds., 2016. *Social inequality in post-growth Japan: transformation during economic and demographic stagnation*. London: Routledge.

de Swaan, J.-C., 2015. Japan's reforms push companies to unlock cash. *Financial Times*, 30 March.

Dore, R.P., 1973. *British factory – Japanese factory: the origins of national diversity in industrial relations*. Berkeley: University of California Press.

Everaert, L. and Ganelli, G., 2016. Japan: time to load a fourth arrow – wage increase. *IMF Direct: The International Monetary Fund's Global Economy Forum*. 13 March. Available from: https://blog-imfdirect.imf.org/2016/03/13/japan-time-to-load-a-fourth-arrow-wage-increases [Accessed 20 October 2016].

Hommerich, C., 2016. The gap as threat: status anxiety in the "middle." *In*: D. Chiavacci and C. Hommerich, eds. *Social inequality in post-growth Japan: transformation during economic and demographic stagnation*. London: Routledge, 37–53.

Hoshi, T. and Kashyap, A.K., 2001. *Corporate financing and governance in Japan: the road to the future*. Harvard: MIT Press.

Ishida, H., 1993. *Social mobility in contemporary Japan: educational credentials, class and the labour market in a cross-national perspective*. London: Macmillan.

Ishizaki, T., 1983. *Nihon no Shotoku to Tomi no Bunpai* [Japan's Income and Wealth Distribution]. Tōkyō: Tōyō Keizai Shinpōsha.

Ito, T., Patrick, H.T., and Weinstein, D.E., eds., 2005. *Reviving Japan's economy: problems and prescriptions*. Cambridge: MIT Press.

Jacoby, S.M., 2005. *The embedded corporation: corporate governance and employment relations in Japan and the United States*. Princeton: Princeton University Press.

Johnson, C., 1982. *MITI and the Japanese miracle: the growth of industrial policy, 1925–1975*. Stanford: Stanford University Press.

Kahn, H., 1970. *The emerging Japanese superstate: challenge and response*. Englewood Cliffs: Prentice-Hall.

Kakei Keizai Kenkyūjo [The Institute for Research on Household Economics], 2015. *Shōhi Seikatsu ni kan suru Paneru Chōsa ni tsuite (Dai 22 Kai Chōsa Kekka)* [Panel Survey on Consumer Behaviour (Results of the 22nd Survey)]. Tōkyō: Kakei Keizai Kenkyūjo.

Lazonick, W., 1991. *Business organization and the myth of the market economy*. New York: Cambridge University Press

Lechevalier, S., 2014. *The great transformation of Japanese capitalism*. London: Routledge.

Lechevalier, S. and Monfort, B., 2016. Abenomics: has it worked? Will it fail? CCJ Discussion Paper Series.

Lincoln, E.J., 2001. *Arthritic Japan: the slow pace of economic reform*. Washington: Brooking Institution Press.

Mainichi Shinbun, 2015a. Bea Saikō Aitsugu: Chūshō Hakyū, Mitoosezu [Successive Salary Increases: Not Reaching Small and Medium Enterprises]. 19 March, morning edition.

Mainichi Shinbun, 2015b. Saitei Chingin, 18 En Hikiage: Saidai Agefuku, Seifu Koshitsu [18 Yen Raise of Basic Income: Government Sticks to Large Increase]. 30 July, morning edition.

Mainichi Shinbun, 2016. Shuntō: 'Kansei' Sanjunme Shissoku, Seikai Keizai Henchō 'Shiome kawatta' [Spring Wage Offensive: 'Governmental Demands' Are Fast Losing Momentum, 'Ocean Current' of World Economy Climate Has Changed]. 17 March, morning edition.

MIAC (Ministry of Internal Affairs and Communications, Statistical Bureau), 2016. *Statistical handbook of Japan 2016*. Tokyo: MIAC.

Mikitani, R. and Posen, A.S., 2000. *Japan's financial crisis and its parallels to US experience*. Washington: Institute for International Economics.

Mulgan, A.G., 2002. *Japan's failed revolution: Koizumi and the politics of economic reform*. Canberra: Asia Pacific Press.

Murata, H., 2015. Jiron Kōron: "2015 Shuntō Kakusa Zesei he no Kadai" [Contemporary Opinion, Public Opinion: "Correction of Inequality a Topic in 2015 Spring Wages Offensive"]. *NHK Kaisetsu Iinshitsu: Kaisetsu Ākaibusu* [News Commentators Bureau: Commentary Archive]. 2 April, Available from: http://www.nhk.or.jp/kaisetsu-blog/100/208672.html [Accessed 20 October 2016].

Nihon Keizai Shinbun, 2015. Abenomikusu Shintō Nakaba: Toshibu to Chihō Hyōka Wareru [Abenomics Half Penetrated: Differences in Valuation in Cities and Countryside]. 23 February, morning edition.

Olcott, G., 2005. *Conflict and change: foreign ownership and the Japanese firm*. Cambridge: Cambridge University Press.

Ouchi, W.G., 1981. *Theory Z: how American business can meet the Japanese challenge*. Reading: Addison-Wesley.

Park, Y.C. and Patrick, H., eds., 2013. *How Finance is shaping the economies of China, Japan, and Korea*. New York: Columbia University Press.

Pascale, R.T. and Athos, A.G., 1981. *The art of Japanese management: applications for American business*. New York: Simon and Schuster.

Pempel, T.J. and Muramatsu, M., 2014. Japanese political studies: where are we? How did we get here? Where are we going? *Japan Forum*, 26 (3), 383–405.

Pesek, W., 2014. *Japanization: what the world can learn from Japan's lost decades*. Singapore: Bloomberg Press.

Porcellacchia, D., 2016. Wage-price dynamics and structural reforms in Japan. IMF Working Paper, WP/16/20.

Prime Minister of Japan and His Cabinet (Ichioku Sōkatsuyaku Kokumin Kaigi, Shushō Kantei), 2015. Ichioku Sōkatsuyaku Shakai no Jitsugen ni mukete Kinkyū ni Jisshi subeki Taisaku: Seichō to Bunbai no Kōjunkan ni Keisei ni mukete [Urgent Policies to Realize a Society in Which All Citizens are Dynamically Engaged: Toward a Positive Cycle of Growth and Distribution]. 26 November. Available from: http://www.kantei.go.jp/jp/singi/ichiokusoukatsuyaku/kinkyu_taisaku/hontai.pdf [Accessed 20 October 2016].

Sako, M., 2006. *Shifting boundaries of the firm: Japanese company - Japanese labour*. Oxford: Oxford University Press.

Shibata, S., 2016. Resisting Japan's neoliberal model of capitalism: intensification and change in contemporary patterns of class struggle. *British Journal of Industrial Relations*, 54 (3), 496–521.

Storz, C., *et al.*, eds., 2013. Asian capitalisms: bringing Asia into the comparative capitalism perspective (special issue). *Socio-Economic Review*, 11 (2).

Sugimoto, Y., 2014. *An introduction to Japanese society*. Cambridge: Cambridge University Press.

Tanabiki, Y. and Miyata, N., 2015. Shigoto no Kachi no Fuchi to Chōteki Henka: "Nihonjin no Ishiki" Chōsa no Niji Bunseki [Structure of the Value of Work and Long-term Change: Secondary Analysis of the "Japanese Consciousness" Survey]. *Shakaigaku Hyōron*, 66 (1), 57–72.

The Economist, 2014. Corporate governance in Japan: a revolution in the making, 3 May.

The Economist, 2015. Japanese companies: winds of change, 6 June.
The Economist, 2016. Japan's economy: three-piece dream suit, 30 July.
Tiberghien, Y., 2007. *Entrepreneurial states: reforming corporate governance in France, Japan, and Korea*. Ithaca: Cornell University Press.
van Houwelingen, P., 2016. Societal pessimism in Japan, the United States, and the Netherlands. *Japanese Journal of Political Science*, 17 (3), 427–450.
Vogel, E.F., 1979. *Japan as number one: lessons for America*. Cambridge: Harvard University Press.
Vogel, S., 2006. *Japan remodeled: how government and industry are reforming Japanese capitalism*. Ithaca: Cornell University Press.
Whittaker, D.H. and Deakin, S., eds., 2009. *Corporate governance and managerial reform in Japan*. Oxford: Oxford University Press.
Witt, M.A., 2006. *Changing Japanese capitalism: societal coordination and institutional adjustment*. Cambridge: Cambridge University Press.
Womack, J.P., Jones, D.T., and Roos, D., 1990. *The machine that changed the world*. New York: Rawson Associates.
Yamada, M., 2004. *Kibō Kakusa Shakai: "Makegumi" no Zetsubōkan ha Nihon o Hikisaku* [Gap Society of Hope: The Despair of the "Looser Group" Is Dividing Japan]. Tōkyō: Chikuma Shobō.

Change and continuity in Japanese corporate reform

MITSUHARU MIYAMOTO

Abstract: Confronted with critical business situations in the late 1990s, Japanese firms began to tackle reforms in both corporate governance and human-resource management. These reforms advocated that Japanese firms shift from being organization-based to market-based corporations, similar to their US counterparts. However, the actual reform did not produce such an overall change but occurred with incremental and cumulative changes within the existing institutional framework. This article examines continuing changes in Japanese firms, and demonstrates that they are diversified into different directions as a result of gradual institutional change.

1. Introduction

Confronted with the difficult business conditions that resulted from the collapse of the economic bubble in the early 1990s, particularly the critical situations of the late 1990s, Japanese firms undertook corporate reforms in two areas: corporate governance and human-resource (HR) management. The former advocated the US-style shareholder-oriented corporate governance, and the latter proposed the US-style market-oriented HR management. Whereas Japanese firms were suffering from a prolonged slump, US firms were being praised for their prosperity due to their shareholder-oriented, market-based corporate system. It therefore seemed apparent to advance a reform modelled on US firms. In fact, many changes have occurred in the Japanese corporate landscape since the late 1990s: the rapid growth of dividends, the adoption of a new style of the board of directors, the decrease in stable employment among regular workers and the increase in short-term employment among non-regular workers – seemingly evidence of the decay of long-term employment (LTE) practice – and the introduction of performance-related pay (PRP) with a widening of the individual pay gap. These looked like a move in the direction of a US-style market-based corporate system.

As Jacoby (2005) pointed out, however, US firms have also moved in a more market-based direction, and thus differences between US and Japanese firms still remain. In fact, as seen later, very few Japanese firms have adopted the US-style corporate governance structure, the so-called 'committee system', in which outside directors are in the majority of the board. Instead, many Japanese firms have preserved the traditional structure, the so-called 'audit board system', in which inside directors still occupy the majority. Similarly, the LTE practice has been preserved despite a large-scale employment reduction and restructuring (Kato 2001, Kambayashi and Kato 2012). Moreover, Japanese firms are clearly far less concerned with stressing shareholder interests, boosting labour mobility, and widening the individual pay gap than are US firms. Therefore, Japanese and US firms are not likely to converge despite the recent changes in Japan.

Viewing the actual change in Japanese firms, particularly the continuity of the LTE practice and the traditional board structure, may reinforce the impression that Japanese firms could not change, at least not drastically change, after all. Although this evidence is likely to show the resilience of the Japanese system, some have expressed disappointment, as if the initial expectations to change had been based on deception (Whittaker and Deakin 2009). This discontent, in turn, aroused an anxious call for radical change, with some arguing that Japanese firms lagged behind US firms due to their resistance to change: in particular, Japanese managers' resistance to shareholder dominance and Japanese workers' resistance to employment flexibility (Noguchi 1995, Yashiro 2009). The target was thus focused on the defeat of their resistance, depriving managerial autonomy and employment security. These calls have been repeated throughout the reform movements of the past two decades, and are now again aroused by 'Abenomics' as if it were a last chance to revive the Japanese economy. As long as US-style corporations have been regarded as the standard model, Japanese firms have been considered to be lagging behind in institutional change.

However, these arguments seem to lose persuasion when viewed in terms of the notion of 'gradual institutional change' presented by Streeck and Thelen (2005) and Mahoney and Thelen (2010). These authors point out the fallacy of advocating overall structural change, such as from an organization-based to market-based corporation, noting that actual change is incremental and cumulative, and that the existing institutional framework changes gradually. In addition, Aoki (2010) discusses the 'evolving diversity in the corporate system', highlighting that the existing system cannot simply be changed into a US-style one; rather, it will evolve into a hybrid system composed of heterogeneous institutions with market-based and organization-based components. Following these points of view, we focus on managerial reform in Japanese firms based the introduction of the corporate executive officer system, an incremental change in the board structure compared with a drastic shift toward the US-style committee system, and investigate how such an incremental change induces a cumulative change in HR practices, and demonstrate the diversification of Japanese firms as a result of gradual institutional change.

First, we view the recent changes in both corporate governance and HR practices. Second, we examine the effects of these changes by referring to the findings of surveys conducted by the Japan Institute for Labour Policy and Training (JILPT) in 2004 and 2008. Third, we demonstrate how Japanese firms are diversified by referring to the estimations of the effects of corporate governance reform. Finally, we present a concluding discussion.

2. Traditional Japanese firm

We begin by reconsidering the nature of the Japanese firm because discussions of reform tend to be one-sided if Japanese firms are misunderstood. As is well-known, Japanese firms have been considered as a model of stakeholder-oriented corporate governance, comprised of organizational HR practices on the one hand, and organizational ownership on the other (Aoki 1988). Although the former has been stylized as 'life-long employment' and 'seniority wage', this view may lead to the misunderstanding that Japanese firms have fallen into rigidity by guaranteeing pay and employment stability. Similarly, stylizing the latter as 'managerial autonomy' may lead to the misunderstanding that Japanese firms are mismanaged by the managerial prerogative. Were this so, Japanese firms could not compete with US firms that are provided with enough flexibility and rationality.

However, organizational HR practices – a tripartite composition of LTE, in-house training and competence-based seniority wages – have formed the basis of the competitiveness of Japanese firms. First, continuous employment allowed continuous training for employees, building organizational competence (Koike 1988). Second, wages were determined according to the appraisal of an individual's competence; thus, wages rose cumulatively with both annual and upgrading rises in competence-rank. Although such a wage increase appeared to be based on seniority, the Japanese wage system was essentially based on both continuous in-house training and successive competence appraisals (Koike 1988, Marsden 1999). This was ultimately sustained on the basis of LTE practice

These long-term perspective HR practices need to be protected from shareholder intervention to pursue short-run interest. This was enabled by ownership structure organized by cross and stable shareholding. Although such protection established managerial autonomy in Japanese firms, it first emerged in US firms – the so-called 'Berle-Means' type managerial firm, due to highly dispersed ownership. However, US managerial firms could not avoid shareholder intervention because the same dispersed ownership activated the market for corporate control (Roe 1994). Thus, for ensuring short-term profits, a short-term employment adjustment was inevitable in US firms. By contrast, Japanese managerial firms have avoided such pressure by organizing shareholders, which served as patient capital for establishing long-term perspective HR management.

In addition, whereas US managerial firms have been subjected to managers' pursuit of their own interests, Japanese ones have been referred to as a 'corporation as a community' (Dore 2000), where managers and employees shared common interests: managerial autonomy on one hand and stable pay and employment on the other. Further, whereas manager's prerogative was paramount in US managerial firms, the voices of Japanese employees have been raised through the Joint-Labour-Management-Committee, which promoted cooperative industrial relations via information sharing in Japanese firms (Kato and Morishima 2002). Furthermore, as mentioned by Aoki (1988), Japanese shareholders enjoyed high rates of return on investments by means of capital gains from increasing stock market prices during the age of managerial firms, from the 1960s to 1980s, compared with the stagnant state of US managerial firms.

Of course, managerial autonomy was not assured in all cases. Aoki (1994) conceptualized as contingent governance, the main banks intervened when loan companies fell into financial crisis and changed the managers to rebuild management. Similarly, in the face of such business difficulties, changes in employment security were inevitable. Even in such cases, however, employment was not reduced simply to ensure a dividend payment. Instead, dividends were cut either before or during cuts in the labour force (Matsuura 2001), and the employment adjustment followed the internal rule between management and unions: stopping new hiring, transferring redundant workers to other jobs or affiliated companies, and terminating non-regular workers' hiring. Although these were devised to assure the regular workers' employment, early retirement was implemented when redundant workers could not be absorbed in this way. It is not unusual to see a large volume of early retirements occur in firms facing a severe downturn. The LTE policy was established on these premises.

Here, the so-called 'dismissal regulation' should be discussed. It is often said that Japanese firms are burdened with excess employment because dismissals are severely restricted by the court, which prescribes strict conditions for dismissal in the form of judicial law. However, judicial law was established in light of the internal rules of employment adjustment mentioned above; dismissals that violate the shared rule are judged to be invalid by the court (Araki 2005). Importantly, early retirement is prescribed as a device for avoiding dismissals in the line of judicial law. Thus, a large volume of early retirements with a special allowance proceeds without serious disputes in the court, although they are actually the same as dismissals in the sense of job losses. Here, we see a case similar to the 'conversion' type of institutional change mentioned by Thelen (2009) and Mahony and Thelen (2010), whereby the existing institution is reinterpreted to fit the new situation. In this case, while the judicial law was originally a device for protecting employment from the abuse of dismissal, it is reinterpreted as a device for justifying employment reduction in the form of early retirement. Therefore, although the adoption of the so-called 'hire and fire' employment practice is impossible in Japanese firms, employment reduction is not necessarily hindered, rather it is implemented following the internal rule.[1]

3. Corporate governance reform

3.1. Banking and managerial crisis

The economic and business environments surrounding Japanese firms have drastically changed since the burst of the bubble economy in the early 1990s, in particular since the banking and managerial crises in the late 1990s. Confronted with these hardships, Japanese firms began to reform in two institutional areas: corporate governance and HR management. Here, we focus on corporate governance reform, and examine HR reform in the next section.

First, stock market conditions have deteriorated significantly: the average rate of annual growth in the Nikkei Stock Average fell drastically from 11.3 per cent during the bubble economy in the 1980s to △5.1 per cent in the 1990s, and △0.3 per cent in the 2000s. By contrast, the average rate of annual growth in Dow Jones Industrial Average rose sharply: from 0.1 per cent in the 1970s to 10.5 per cent in the 1980s and 12.9 per cent in the 1990s, although it fell to 0.4 per cent in the 2000s due to the disturbance caused by the collapse of Lehman Brothers. Considering that US firms shifted from a focus on managerial autonomy to shareholder-oriented corporate governance during the 1980s due to the stock market pressure provoked by the previous stagnant position (Gordon 2007), it seemed natural to suppose that Japanese firms would be forced to move toward a shareholder orientation due to the extremely stagnant state of the stock markets during the 1990s and 2000s, the so-called 'lost two decades'.

From this perspective, we see two factors that accelerated the corporate governance reform: liquidation in the stock markets due to the dissolution of cross and stable shareholdings on one hand, and a managerial crisis due to the critically declining profits on the other. The former was triggered by the banking crisis in the late 1990s and was accelerated by the change in accounting rule, from an acquisition-value to a market-value basis. These two factors forced the main banks to release the stocks they owned, which had been the basis of cross and stable shareholdings, and a large part of the relinquished stock was acquired by foreign investors. On a market-value basis, foreign investors' shareholdings were 4.7 per cent of the Tokyo Stock Exchange (TSE) in 1990; this increased to 18.8 per cent in 2000, and to 31.7 per cent in 2014, making foreign investors as a whole the largest block shareholders in 'Japan-Inc.'.

There is no reason for foreign investors to behave as patient capital, like organized shareholders. They not only affect stock prices with their high number of deals according to quarterly profits (accounting for about 70 per cent of total trading in the TSE First and Second), but also act as activist shareholders to require the increase in dividends, change in corporate strategy, and the adoption of a US-style corporate governance structure. These concerns have been raised not only through the annual shareholders meeting but also through the threat of hostile takeover by aggressive hedge funds. No hostile takeover has yet succeeded because corporations still maintain cross-shareholdings, accounting for 21.3 per cent in 2014, but Japanese firms realized that they were surrounded by aggressive shareholders, which led to corporate governance reform to cope with shareholder pressure.

Another factor that accelerated corporate governance reform was the profitability crisis in Japanese firms around 2000. As shown in Figure 1, which depicts firms with more than one billion yen in capital, corporate profits declined rapidly after the economic bubble burst. They fell to a critical level during the banking crisis in the late 1990s, and declined further in the early 2000s due to the economic downturn caused by the failure of many US dot-coms. Japanese firms faced unprecedented managerial crises; not only the fear of bankruptcy, seen in several large banks and companies, but also the absence of any rescue from the main banks, which had been expected in order to rebuild management. In fact, Nissan, Japan's second-largest automobile company, was forced to merge with Renault, and Sogo, Japan's largest department store, was forced to declare bankruptcy. In both cases, their main bank, the Industrial Bank of Japan (IBJ), no longer had the financial ability to rebuild these companies. Rather, the IBJ had itself fallen into financial crisis and had to merge with other banks to survive. As with the stock market pressures, Japanese firms realized that there would be no rescue in the event of a business crisis, which led to corporate governance reform to rebuild management through their own efforts.

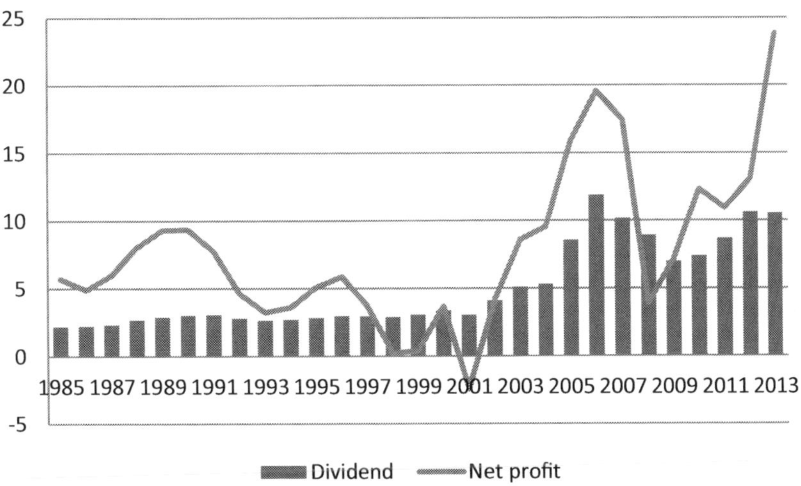

Figure 1 Trend of net profits and dividend payments (real-term, a trillion yen)
Source: Business Outlook Survey (Ministry of Finance)
Note: Non-financial companies with more than one billion yen in capital

3.2. *Increase in dividends and introduction of the executive officer system*

First, we can see the change in corporate governance in the rapid growth of dividends beginning in the early 2000s, as shown in Figure 1. It contrasts strikingly with the low and constant trend before 2000, during the economic bubble in the 1980s, despite increasing profits, and during the 'lost decade' of the 1990s, despite decreasing profits. This was called the 'stable dividend policy', which intended to avoid shareholder intervention by maintaining a certain level of dividends during bad periods and keeping it in reserve during good periods. Such a policy changed, and dividends became highly correlated with profits; rapidly decreasing with the sharp decline in profits during the downturn after the global financial crisis in 2008, yet remaining at a significantly higher level than the previous level before 2000. Thus, from the viewpoint of dividend policies, corporate governance moved toward a shareholder orientation.

Executive pay also changed along with increasing dividends, as shown in Table 1, demonstrating the correlation coefficients among pre-tax profits, dividends, executive pay and employment pay for firms with more than one billion yen in capital. Before the dividend policy changed, from 1992 to 2001, there was a very strong correlation between executive and employee pay; both shared a common pay system on the internal ladder. After the dividend policy changed, however, from 2002 to 2011, the correlation disappeared, and executive pay as well as dividends became correlated with profits; executive managers were separated from employees and made conscious of their responsibility for profits.[2] In this way, not only dividend policy but also the relationship between managers and employees changed under increasing shareholder pressure.

Next, worsening business performance, another factor in corporate governance reform, led to a change in the managerial organization through the introduction of the corporate executive officer system. It is well known that the board of

Table 1 Correlations with profits (non-financial firms with more than one billion yen in capital)

Correlation coefficient				
1992–2001	Pretax profits	Dividend	Executive pay	Employee pay
Pretax profit	1			
Dividends	–0.3161	1		
Executive pay	0.1353	0.3172	1	
Employee pay	0.2954	0.2688	0.9673*	1
2002–2011				
Pretax profit	1			
Dividend	0.7122*	1		
Executive pay	0.6972*	0.5118	1	
Employee pay	0.1942	–0.2736	0.3869	1

*significant at 5% level
Note: Both executive and employee pay excluding bonuses

directors in the traditional Japanese firm had many members, as senior managers of business units were also nominated as directors. Thus, the function of the board was, in effect, to approve the business decisions presented by unit managers. This was referred to as a 'bottom-up' style of decision-making and was appreciated because it promoted close coordination between top and middle managers. Nevertheless, strategic decisions such as the restructuring of existing business tended to be delayed, and unit managers' accountability tended to be obscure. For these reasons, the executive officer system was introduced, in which unit managers were separated from board members, were nominated as executive officers, provided with the power and responsibility to achieve unit performance, and supervised by the board of directors. According to Kubo (2010), among the 189 companies in the Nikkei Stock Average Index, 29 (15.3 per cent) had adopted the corporate executive officer system by 1999, and 122 (64.6 per cent) had done so by 2005.

Amid the growth in dividends and the introduction of the executive officer system, Japanese firms appeared to shift to the US-style corporate governance structure. In fact, a new corporate law was enacted in 2005 to promote the adoption of the US-style board structure – the 'company with committee' – whereby independent outside directors become the majority on the board and supervise management via the three committees that handled nomination, compensation and auditing. Japanese firms were provided with the same institutional apparatus as were US firms.

However, very few Japanese firms have actually adopted the committee system. According to a TSE survey, only 42 companies in the TSE Frist had adopted it by 2012, roughly 10 years after the new corporate law was introduced (Tokyo Stock Exchange 2013). An overwhelming majority of Japanese firms continued to use the traditional structure, 'company with audit board', in which the board is composed of the majority of internal directors without a committee, and supervised by an audit board including at least one independent auditor (now, two independent auditors). This does not imply the avoidance of change. Instead of adopting the committee system, Japanese firms advanced the board reform in the direction of reducing the number of board members, by which it was intended to strengthen the board's decision-making. According to the aforementioned survey, the average number of directors was drastically reduced from 21.4 persons in 1997 to 8.7 in 2012. However, the average number of independent directors was very low: only 0.7 in a 'company with audit board', whereas 3.9 in a 'company with committee'.

These observations may imply a delay or insufficiency in corporate governance reform in Japan. In particular, a very small number of independent directors is considered to be ineffective in supervising management with regard to shareholder interest, and an evidence that Japanese firms preserve managerial autonomy against that interest; therefore, foreign investors' attacks have always been focused on it. Thus, confronted with increasing pressures, the Financial Service

Agency and TSE announced the Corporate Governance Code in 2014 to promote the nomination of at least two independent directors. Although this was a voluntary code, it had a compulsory effect due to the attachment of the Comply or Explain Rule. As a result, many firms rushed to nominate independent directors; according to the latest data, the share of firms having more than two independent directors in the TSE First increased drastically, from 21.5 per cent in 2014, via 48.4 per cent in 2015, and to 77.9 per cent in 2016 (Tokyo Stock Exchange 2016).

In the course of this change, corporate law was again amended in such a way as to allow a new board structure: the 'company with audit/supervisory committee'. It has only an audit committee composed of two independent directors; in other words, it is distinct from the 'company with committee' by the absence of the nomination/compensation committee. The 'company with committee' is now called the 'company with nomination/compensation committee' despite having an audit committee in order to distinguish it from a new one. Then, many firms (357 firms in the TSE First, according to a survey of JACD (Japan Association of Corporate Directors (2016)), moved to this new board style by sliding the two independent auditors in the original 'company with audit board' to the directors of the new 'company with audit/supervisory committee'. It was a very convenient way because it was adequate to nominate the same person as a new director. In sum, a loophole was created to meet the corporate governance code. By contrast, the traditional 'company with audit board' holds at least two independent directors and auditors, which is still the majority in Japanese firms.

Here, we see the three types of corporation: traditional audit board type, nomination/compensation type, and the latest audit/supervisory type. These three types are statutory under corporate law, and their decisions are binding on management. On the other hand, however, many firms among the traditional audit board type are establishing a nomination and compensation committee voluntarily: totalling 546 firms according to the aforementioned JACD survey. In these firms, a committee's decisions do not have a compulsory but an advisory effect on management. Final decisions depend on the board, comprised of a majority of inside directors. In short, Japanese firms change as the need arises, but discretionally. However, the nomination/compensation type, having been recommended as a US-type corporation, still has only 61 firms on the TSE First even in 2016.

In this way, we can see a gradual institutional change in Japanese firms, not overall but incrementally within the existing institutional framework, while introducing the executive officer system and reducing the board members by nominating at least two independent directors on one hand, yet preserving the traditional board structure without the formal committee of nomination and compensation on the other. This was neither a delay nor an insufficiency in corporate governance reform because Japanese firms intrinsically did not intend to become more like their US counterparts. As mentioned by Buchanan and Deakin

(2009), this was done to enable the managerial organization as a whole to work more effectively, especially with regard to strengthening strategic management. Thus, independent directors were not excluded from the outset; rather, they had already been introduced as advisors to management. Therefore, the above code may be accepted without significant resistance, and even a nomination committee was established voluntarily in the form of advisory committee.

In short, Japanese firms have adopted their own corporate governance structure, one that is distant from shareholder dominance. As Gordon (2007) pointed out, in US firms, outside directors were first regarded as having an advisory function, which transformed into a monitoring function during the 1980s, and eventually became the norm during the 1990s, with the establishment of shareholder-dominated corporate governance. However, as argued by Mayer (2013), corporate governance should have a varied form. Contrary to the dominant view of shareholder primacy, he argues that, if a corporation works in a stable and sustainable way in a society, it is necessary to make commitment to various stakeholders, and so it is necessary to establish the independence of the board from shareholders. Put bluntly, the role of corporate governance is not only to protect shareholder interest from managerial prerogative, but also to protect the corporation from shareholders' pressure to pursue the short-term interest. This has been the notion of Japanese firms, as seen in a popular phrase of the 'corporation as a societal institution'. Therefore, Japanese managers are more likely to be punished for violating this notion than for poor performance. This is not to deny shareholder interest. Rather, it is necessary to reply to shareholder's demands in order to maintain the independence of the board. From this standpoint, Japanese firms have increased dividends and have struggled to rebuild management for improving performance. This has been conducted by internally promoted managers, even in firms with a committee of nomination. Although new managers were nominated in the traditional way, only a few individual with non-traditional backgrounds, such as from overseas branches or affiliated companies, were selected as top managers. These new managers initiated reforms as a quasi-outsiders by cutting off the past internal connections (Olcott 2009).

4. Work organization reform

4.1. Introduction of performance-related pay

After the economic bubble burst, the urgent issue for Japanese firms was restoring the corporate performance. As mentioned, the first task was to reform managerial organization to strengthen strategic management, which led to the introduction of the executive officer system. This in turn proceeded to the reform of work organization in order to implement these managerial strategies. Then, PRP was introduced in order to promote employees' work motivation. Here, we see that the introduction of the executive officer system as a reform of managerial organization

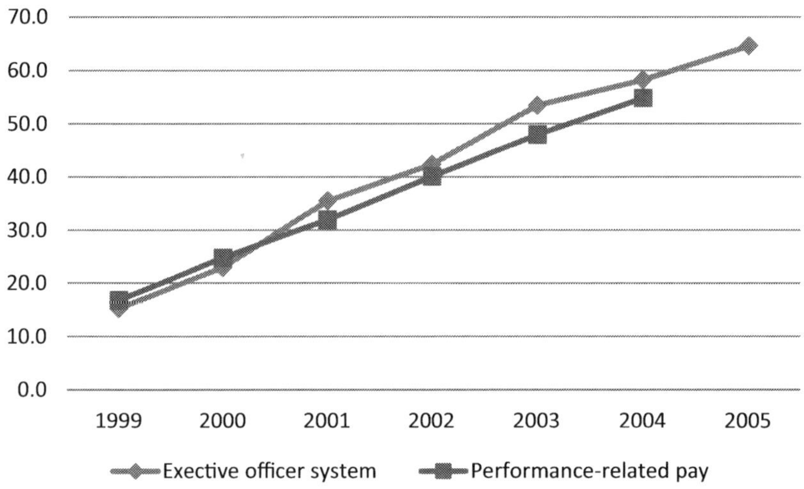

Figure 2 Cumulative rate of the introduction of the executive officer system and performance-related pay
Source: Executive officer system is Kubo (2010), performance-related pay is JILTP (2007)

and the introduction of PRP as a reform of work organization proceeded in parallel, as shown in Figure 2. The data on the executive officer system rely on Kubo (2010), including 189 companies in the Nikkei Stock Average Index, and PRP on the JILPT survey (JILPT 2007), including 1280 firms. While the two are drawn from aggregate data, they will be analysed as a causality in the next section by referring to the estimation of the effect of board reform on PRP introduction.

From another point of view, Japanese firms were keenly aware of the defects of the existing wage system by facing sharply declining profits. As mentioned, the system was designed to determine wages according to the appraisals of individual competence. However, it was difficult to actually implement this evaluation, which in effect became seniority-based evaluation by relying on the appraisals of incumbent's experience. Therefore, both annual and upgrading wage rises became related to the length of service. Labour costs, therefore, increase as age increases. Further, this system was seen to discourage work motivation due to small differentials in the actual wages. For these reasons, instead of the existent competence-rank system, a performance-rank system was introduced not only to curb the increasing labour costs by diminishing the annual rise relying on experience appraisals, but also to stimulate the employees' motivation by widening individual pay gaps according to short-term performance appraisals (Tsuru *et al.* 2005, Ishida and Higuchi 2009).[3] Further, along with the introduction of PRP, HR practices were also changed: boosting early promotion, recruiting mid-career managers, and demoting poorly performed employees. These practices, referred to as 'strategic HR management', correspond to strategic management intended by the executive officer system.

However, as soon as PRP was introduced, there was a focus on its failures rather than its successes. While various debates emerged about the PRP scheme, the central issue was the short-term performance appraisal. It was apparent that this approach contradicted the notion of skill formation in Japanese firms, which depends on long-term in-house training and corresponding long-term competence appraisals. Further, as discussed concerning the so-called 'multi-task problem' (Holmstrom and Milgrom 1991), it became apparent that, as PRP stressed the achievement of individual performance, employees' contribution to unmeasurable factors such as the organization's overall performance and the challenge of tackling difficult tasks tended to be neglected (Morishima 1999, Marsden 2009, Miyamoto and Nohara 2013).

For these reasons, the work of PRP was soon modified. For instance, whereas the performance-rank system was applied to managerial-class workers, the competence-rank system was preserved for non-managerial workers in the process of skill development. Similarly, competence appraisals were added to performance appraisals for managerial-class workers because of the difficulty in evaluating the contributions to the overall organizational performance (Ishida and Higuchi 2009). In addition, performance appraisals were modified in the direction of the long-perspective by evaluating the process to achieve the outcome. These modifications result in the restraint of wage variations and differentials that would be generated by the short-term performance appraisals.

In this way, the PRP scheme is mitigated contrary to the initial presumption that employee motivation is stimulated by widening the pay gap. For instance,

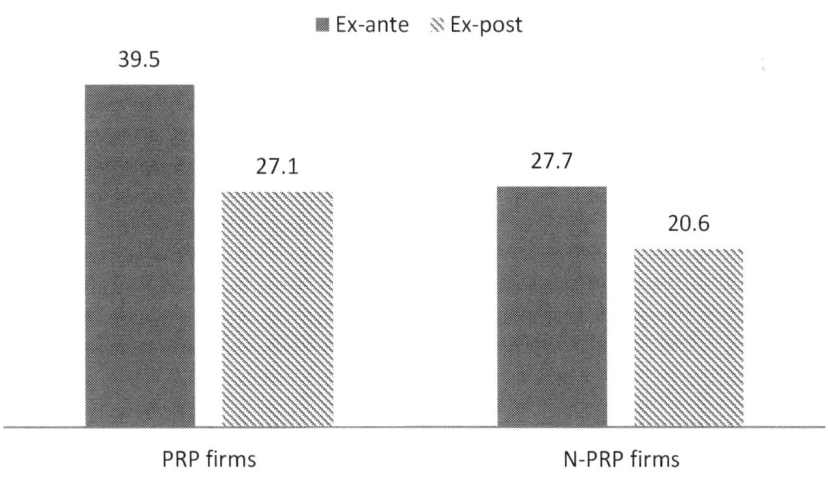

Figure 3 Wage differentials: comparison between PRP and N-PRP firms
Source: JILPT (2007)
Note: Wage differentials are the range between the maximum and minimum paid to the section managers with the average being fixed as 100. PRP firms are those that introduced PRP, N-PRP firms are those that did not introduced. Ex-ante denotes the designed differentials, and ex-post denotes the actual.

we can demonstrate the actual operation of PRP on the pay gap, as shown in Figure 3, referring to the aforementioned JILPT survey (JILPT 2007, Miyamoto and Nohara 2013). Here, the wage differentials are measured as the range between the maximum and minimum wage paid to section managers, with the average being fixed at 100, between the ex-ante differential that is designated on the pay table and the ex-post differential that is actually paid, and between the firms that introduced PRP (PRP firms) and those that did not (N-PRP firms). For the PRP-firms, although the ex-ante differential on average is in the range of 40, the ex-post differential is around 27 (a 33 per cent reduction). Interestingly, the ex-post differential in the PRP firms is nearly equal to the ex-ante differential in the N-PRP firms. In other words, although wage differentials are designated in the traditional organizations (N-PRP firms), such differentials are not realized; rather, they are realized when PRP is introduced, but on a reduced scale.

We thus observe that the operation of PRP is weakened eventually. One perspective is that such a weakened PRP scheme fails to stimulate work motivations and that Japanese firms therefore remain stagnant despite the introduction of PRP. A contrasting perspective is that such a modification may be a supplementary condition for the PRP scheme to be accepted by employees. In general, PRP is supposed to come into conflict with the employees' existing psychological contract (Rousseau 1995), particularly the expectation of pay and employment stability. If the operation of PRP destroys an existing psychological contract, and/or a new psychological contract is not shaped, employees would resist PRP or be demotivated. On the contrary, PRP seems to be accepted without such resistance, perhaps because restraints are put on it, such as the preservation of competence appraisals, mitigating individual differentials, and maintaining LTE, as discussed below. In short, as in the case of board reform, we observe not an overall but a gradual change in the Japanese wage system: a move from a system comprised of competence and seniority to one of competence and performance. This also displays a gradual institutional change, wherein new elements are modified to be integrated into old ones. Thus, a new institution was established as a hybrid structure composed of new and old elements.

4.2. Decline in long-term employment?

We have examined the reform of work organization focusing on the introduction of PRP. Now, we discuss the change in LTE practice. Alongside the prolonged depression and the increasing pressure to stress shareholder interest, LET practice has been met with pessimism. As long as the US-style corporate governance was the model, it seemed inevitable that shareholder interests would be given priority over employment stability. Even though such a shareholder model is not adopted, board reform is likely to weaken the employment stability because it boosts the restructuring of the existing business accompanied with a large volume of employment reduction. Similarly, if board reform strengthens the PRP scheme to stimulate the individual motivation, it may intensify the pressure to expel the underperforming employees.

On the contrary, an oft-cited survey shows a contrast between Japanese and US firms facing declining performance (Yoshimori 1997): whereas 97.1 per cent of Japanese firms listed employment as their priority, 89.2 per cent of US firms listed dividends as their priority. Although this survey very clearly demonstrated the nature of traditional Japanese firms, it was conducted in 1991, before the economic downturn due to the burst of the bubble economy. Thus, Matsuura (2001) extended the data from 1991 to 1997, during which Japanese firms faced many hardships. He estimated the behaviour of firms with deficits for two successive periods, and discovered that 52.5 per cent of the sample firms cut both dividends and employment, 43.6 per cent cut dividends only, and 1.8 per cent cut employment only. Kubo (2011) extended the data from 1996 to 2009, when corporate governance reform actually proceeded, and discovered that the probability of employment cuts due to worsening profits increased in the later period (2002 to 2009) compared with the earlier period (1996 to 2001). Employment cuts also increased in firms that were reforming corporate governance with a relatively high ratio of foreign investors. These findings correspond with Ahmadjian and Robbins (2005), who found that the restructuring of existing business was accelerated in firms with higher ratios of foreign shareholdings. However, Kubo (2011) showed that 9.8 per cent of the sample firms chose to cut employment only, even between 2002 and 2009.

According to these findings, LTE policy seems to have continued under recent corporate governance reform as well as the prolonged depression, while the traditional view that gave priority to employment over dividends did not continue. Although the number of regular workers covered by LTE practice has rapidly decreased due to the long-lasting depression, Kato (2001) and Kambayashi and Kato (2012) found that the 10-year retention rate of employees aged 30 to 44 has not declined. Similarly, in spite of the acceleration of restructuring, the employment adjustment process has been preserved. Although early retirement frequently occurs, it follows the internal agreement between management and unions. If this is breached, as in the case of PRP, employees' psychological contract is destroyed, and resistance to restructuring is provoked. LTE practice will thus continue as long as Japanese firms consider that an effective work organization relies on stable employment relations, although this has produced another problem about differentials between regular and non-regular workers.

To summarize the discussion up to here, we first identified two factors leading to corporate governance reform: increasing shareholder pressure due to the liquidation of stock markets, and managerial crisis due to a significant decline in corporate profits, both resulting from the banking crisis in the late 1990s. Second, in response to these factors, two changes occurred in managerial organization: the rapid growth of dividends and the introduction of the executive officer system, both of which began in parallel in the early 2000s. Third, PRP and other strategic HR practices were introduced along with a continuing board reform that intended to strengthen strategic management. Finally, LTE practice seemed to be maintained throughout these reforms.

Here, we observe the change in and continuity of Japanese firms in the course of corporate reforms. The rapid growth of dividends is likely perceived as a shift toward a shareholder orientation, whereas a board structure that preserves managerial autonomy reflects the continuity of the traditional Japanese firms. Similarly, the introduction of PRP indicates a change toward market-based HR practices, whereas the maintenance of the LTE policy reflects the continuity of traditional organization-based HR practices. In this way, Japanese firms combine different institutions into a hybrid structure: market-based corporate governance and organization-based LTE practice on one hand, and organization-based LTE and market-based PRP practice on the other. However, these combinations are not reflected in the same way across Japanese firms. Instead, Japanese firms have moved in different directions along with both corporate governance and HR reforms. Below, the considerations so far are examined using the survey data and investigated in terms of the diversification of Japanese firms.

5. Empirical findings on the corporate reform

This section examines the corporate reform by referring to the two surveys conducted by JILPT in 2004 and 2008 (JILPT 2007, Miyamoto 2016), producing 1280 replies in 2004, 923 replies in 2008, and 235 matched firms, both from a population of 18,000 firms with more than 200 employees. The 2004 survey examined how Japanese firms have changed in their corporate governance and HR practices amid the business hardships that occurred after the banking crisis in the late 1990s. The 2008 survey, conducted just before the collapse of Lehman Brothers, examined how these changes were revised during the rapid recovery that took place from 2003 to 2007. Thus, the survey asked about changes that had occurred during the previous five years.

We present below the key findings on corporate governance and HR practices. First, we asked three questions about corporate governance; how has your firm emphasized the following three managerial issues – increasing the shareholder value, conducting board reform such as introducing the executive officer system, and respecting the CSR concerns. Table 2 shows the ratio of the 'emphasis' answer to the three questions. In the 2004 survey, about half of the listed firms gave an emphasis answer to increasing shareholder value (shareholder orientation), and conducting board reform; both responses increased by more than half in the 2008 survey. However, these responses were naturally low among the non-listed firms. Moreover, as for respecting the CSR concerns (CSR orientation),

Table 2 Three dimensions of corporate governance reform

Management issues in the previous five years (percentage of 'emphasis' answer)				
	2004		2008	
	Listed	Non-listed	Listed	Non-listed
Shareholder orientation	55.2	11.0	64.9	16.1
Board reform	46.3	19.6	51.0	29.4
CSR orientation	64.9	56.5	76.6	62.2

most of the listed and non-listed firms placed managerial emphasis on this in both the 2004 and 2008 surveys.

These results clearly indicate the changes in corporate governance mentioned above. The emphasis answer to increasing shareholder value likely corresponds to the rapid growth of dividends since the early 2000s. Similarly, an emphasis on conducting board reform likely corresponds to the increasing introduction of the executive officer system. In addition, a high ratio emphasizing the CSR concern likely reflects the recent popularity of CSR. Now, many Japanese firms publish the two annual reports: corporate governance and CSR. However, one question arises: how are the two reports consistent? Isn't it contradictory? As discussed later, CSR is associated with the two types of corporate governance: shareholder and stakeholder-oriented. If CRS in Japanese firms relates to stakeholder orientation, shareholder orientation in the first question has to be reinterpreted. These are discussed below through the several estimations of corporate governance variables.

Second, Table 3 shows the responses to the LTE and PRP practice. Concerning LTE policy, we included three responses: 'maintaining LTE for regular workers', 'restricting LTE to core workers' and 'abandoning LTE practice'. Whereas the first response indicates a continuation of the traditional LTE practice (i.e. maintaining LTE for almost all regular workers), the second response divides

Table 3 LTE and PRP practices

Survey by JILPT				
	2004		2008	
	Listed	Non-listed	Listed	Non-listed
Maintaining LTE for regular workers	71.8	69.4	83.3	79.3
Restricting LTE to core workers	19.5	21.8	12.5	16.0
Abandoning LTE	8.7	8.8	4.2	4.7
Introducing PRP	69.9	55.9	71.9	52.8
Widening pay gap	72.4	59.4	51.5	42.3

regular workers into core and non-core workers and restricts LTE to core workers. Thus, the second response is regarded as a step toward abandoning LTE policy, while the third response does so explicitly.

Almost 70 per cent of respondent firms had maintained LTE policy for regular workers, about 20 per cent had restricted LTE to core workers, and nearly 10 per cent had abandoned LTE in the 2004 survey. The ratio of firms that maintained the LTE policy increases in the 2008 survey, probably due to the economic recovery, and the ratios that restricted or abandoned LTE policy correspondingly decrease. Regarding PRP policy, on the other hand, we asked about its introduction, and whether the pay gap for the section chief was widening. About 70 per cent of the listed firms and about 55 per cent of the non-listed firms had introduced PRP in the 2004 survey. However, there is no significant difference in the ratios between the 2004 and 2008 surveys. Rather, the widening pay gap ratio decreased. In contrast to the LTE policy, the introduction of PRP appears to be rather sluggish.

We can thus confirm that a large number of Japanese firms have preserved their LTE policy despite the long-lasting economic downturn. At the same time, however, a shift from the traditional LTE policy is observed; about 30 per cent in 2004 and about 20 per cent in 2008 of respondent firms, including both restricting and abandoning LTE.[4] Then, we classified the respondent firms into four types based on the combination of LTE and PRP, as shown in Figure 4. The firms that maintained LTE and did not introduce PRP (N-PRP) are classified as 'traditional-J type', while the firms that maintained LTE and introduced PRP are classified as 'new-J type'. The firms that did not maintain LTE (N-LTE: both restriction and abandonment of LTE) and introduced PRP are classified as 'A type', while the firms that neither maintained LTE nor introduced PRP are classified as 'declined-J type'. In the 2004 survey, the traditional-J type accounted for only 30 per cent, whereas the new-J type accounted for about 40 per cent, the A type accounted for about 20 per cent, and the declined-J type accounted for

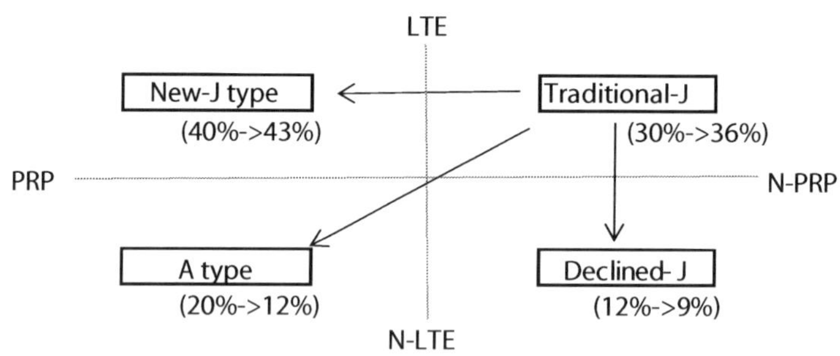

Figure 4 Diversification in Japanese firms
Note: N-LTE denotes the policy of both restricting and abandoning LTE. N-PRP denotes the policy of not introducing PRP. Parentheses show the percentage of each type: left is 2004, right is 2008.

about 10 per cent. In the 2008 survey, the ratio of both new-J and traditional-J types increased, and the ratio of both A and declined-J types decreased, because the ratio of firms that maintained LTE increased, while the ratio of firms that introduced PRP remained nearly the same.

As shown in Figure 4, the traditional-J and A types are contrasting, and the new-J type is categorized as a hybrid type combining different institutional approaches, such as organization-based LTE and market-based PRP.[5] Further, the declined-J type implies the degeneration of the traditional-J type. A similar classification was demonstrated by Jackson and Miyajima (2007), who classified 723 firms listed on the TSE in 2002 on three dimensions – market-based corporate governance or not, maintaining LTE or not, and introducing PRP or not – and presented six types of Japanese firms. A combination of market-based (shareholder-oriented) corporate governance, maintaining LTE, and introducing PRP is categorized as the hybrid type, referred to as 'Japanese blue-chip firms'. Although Jackson and Miyajima (2007) provided a comprehensive classification, it still remains within the typology. By contrast, we investigate how such diversity evolved from the traditional Japanese firms by examining the effects of corporate governance reform.

Thus, we estimated the effects of the three corporate governance variables (i.e. shareholder orientation, board reform, and CSR orientation) on the LTE and PRP practices, and on the diversification of Japanese firms. As the three corporate variables are endogenously affected (both shareholder and CSR orientations positively affect board reform), we estimated them step-by-step, examining the cross-effects between them. Here, we demonstrate the estimation results only for the three variables, controlling for the other variables such as profit rate, number of employees, industry dummy, and listed dummy, and other related variables such as the degree of employment reduction and the ratio of non-regular employment for LTE policy (a full description is given by Miyamoto (2016)).

Tables 4 and 5 shows the effects on LTE and PRP policy, respectively. We distinguished the restricting and abandoning LTE policies as being categorically different; thus, we estimated the effects on the three policies in two steps. First, we run a logit estimation for the first policy (maintaining LTE = 1, otherwise = 0), next, a multi-logit estimation for the probability of the second (restricting LTE) and the third (abandoning LTE) policy to be chosen compared with the first policy. Similarly, we estimated the effects on PRP policy, using a logit estimation (introducing PRP = 1, otherwise = 0).

The estimation results show that, first, shareholder orientation does not affect LTE policy, whereas it positively affects PRP introduction. Second, board reform negatively affects LTE policy, tends to restrict LTE to core workers, and positively and strongly affects PRP introduction, as expected from the co-proceeding of the executive officer system and PRP introduction. Third, CSR orientation has a strongly positive effect on maintaining LTE for regular workers.

Table 4 Estimations of LTE practices

Estimation (1) Logit estimation (maintaining LTET = 1, otherwise = 0) Estimation (2) Multi-logit estimation (base category is Maintaining LTE)			
	2004		
	(1)	(2)	
Independent variables	Maintaining	Restricting	Abandoning
Shareholder orientation	0.002	0.040	0.361
Board reform	–0.294*	0.408**	0.355
CSR orientation	0.418***	–0.325*	–0.658***
Number of observations	1009	1006	
Log likelihood	–591.931	–762.874	
Pseudo R^2	0.029	0.030	
	2008		
	(1)	(2)	
Independent variables	Maintaining	Restricting	Abandoning
Shareholder orientation	–0.346	0.415	0.141
Board reform	–0.29	0.461**	–0.3
CSR orientation	0.468**	–0.201	–1.308***
Number of observations	706	709	
Log likelihood	–338.887	–406.015	
Pseudo R^2	0.020	0.043	

Note: Other control variables are omitted from the table.
*$p<0.10$, **$p<0.05$, ***$p<0.01$

Table 5 Estimation of PRP practice

Logit estimation (introducing PRP = 1, otherwise = 0)		
Independent variables	2004	2008
Shareholder orientation	0.343*	0.346*
Board reform	0.528***	0.502***
CSR orientation	–0.0257	0.469***
Number of observations	1055	738
Log likelihood	–688.279	–484.047
Pseudo R^2	0.036	0.049

Note: Other control variables are omitted from the table.
*$p<0.10$, **$p<0.05$, ***$p<0.01$

Table 6 Estimation of the diversity of Japanese firms

Estimation (1) Logit estimation (Traditional-J = 1, otherwise = 0)
Estimation (2) Multi-logit estimation (base category is the Traditional-J type

	2004			
	(1)	(2)		
Independent variables	Traditional-J	New-J	A	Declined-J
Shareholder-orientation	–0.480**	0.493**	0.292	0.425
Board reform	–0.719***	0.683***	0.836***	0.600**
CSR-orientation	0.114	0.0648	–0.464**	–0.255
Number of observations	1050	1053		
Log Likelihood	–617.736	–1312.09		
Pseudo R^2	0.0382	0.0271		

	2008			
	(1)	(2)		
Independent variables	Traditional-J	New-J	A	Declined-J
Shareholder-orientation	–0.370*	0.306	0.647**	0.262
Board reform	–0.420**	0.419**	0.772***	–0.0155
CSR-orientation	–0.238	0.473***	0.0359	–0.630**
Number of observations	733	736		
Log Likelihood	–472.840	–833.383		
Pseudo R^2	0.0281	0.0375		

Note: Other control variables are omitted from the table.
$^{*}p<0.10$, $^{**}p<0.05$, $^{***}p<0.01$

These results represent important findings and confirm our considerations in the previous sections. First, although shareholder orientation promotes board reform to achieve higher profits for dividends, this does not imply the shareholder primacy in the sense that stable employment is denied for the stake of shareholder interests. In other words, increasing dividends is thought to be compatible with LTE policy. Second, it is board reform that really creates changes in Japanese firms; it restricts LTE to core workers and promotes PRP introduction. This is because board reform strengthens strategic management; thus, LTE policy tends to be restricted to core workers who are expected to contribute to managerial strategies on one hand, and PRP is introduced to motivate them to achieve those strategies on the other. Third, by contrast, it is CSR orientation that sustains LTE policy for almost all regular workers. In this sense, CSR orientation works as a proxy of stakeholder orientation. Here, we see the two contrasting effects on LTE: one is a negative effect via board reform, the other is a positive effect via CSR orientation. Thus, LTE policy depends on which one is more effective. At least up to now, the effect of CSR orientation exceeds that of board reform.

It should be noted that CSR concern is not necessarily related to employment stability or stakeholder-oriented corporate governance. Rather, CSR is likely more activated in US firms than in Japanese firms; however, CSR does not relate to LTE policy in US firms. As mentioned by Tirole (2001), corporate governance and CSR are dichotomous in the US and the UK; corporate governance is oriented toward shareholder primacy, whereas CSR is oriented toward the 'stakeholder society'. For instance, in UK firms, CSR is referred to as providing a donation to training facilities for unemployed persons expelled by shareholder-oriented corporate governance (Kinderman 2012). That is to say, employees are outside the scope of CSR concern in the UK and the US. By contrast, in Japan, employees are included in the CSR concern and covered by LTE policy as a 'stakeholder company'. This finding also supports the VoC (variety of capitalism) approach to CSR (Brammer *et al.* 2012); CSR is complementary with the stakeholder-oriented corporate governance in coordinated market economies, such as Germany and Japan, whereas, in liberal market economies, such as the US and the UK, CSR is substitutionary to shareholder-oriented corporate governance. It used to be common, as a notion of a community firm, to say that corporate responsibility for Japanese firms was to secure employment stability. Although this has been criticized for being an out-of-date management style by the advocates of shareholder-oriented corporate governance, this old notion has been survived by CSR orientation, while the original advocate, Dore (2009), now has a pessimistic view of it.

Further, by integrating these findings, we estimated the effects on the diversification of Japanese firms. We conducted two-step estimations: first, a logit estimation for the traditional-J type (traditional-J = 1, otherwise = 0), next, a multi-logit estimation for the remaining types, new-J, A, and declined-J, based on the traditional-J type. As shown in Table 6, the traditional-J type is reduced when shareholder orientation is strengthened and board reform is advanced, which corresponds to the previous findings that the traditional Japanese firms declined alongside corporate governance reform. Next, the new-J and A types are diversified from the traditional-J type by the effect of board reform that restricts LTE and introduces PRP, and the new-J and A types are diversified from one another by the effect of CSR orientation that maintains LTE: negative effect on the A type in 2004, and positive effect on the new-J type in 2008.

Finally, Figure 5 depicts the process of diversification in Japanese firms. First, we started with the two factors that enforced corporate governance reform around 2000: increasing shareholder pressure due to the dissolution of cross and stable shareholdings and managerial crisis due to the critically declining profits. The former resulted in the increase in dividends, and the latter urged the rebuilding of managerial organization. The former led to shareholder orientation with

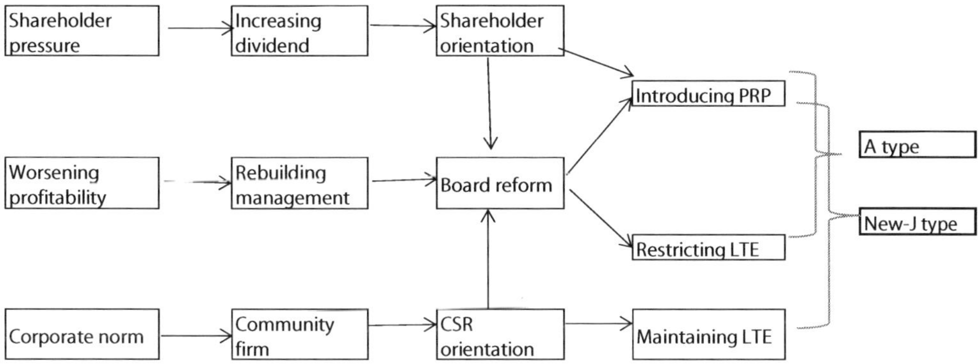

Figure 5 Process of the diversification

the increase in dividends, and the latter led to board reform with the introduction of the executive officer system. On the other hand, the notion of the community firm was preserved in an awareness of CSR concerns along with recent reforms, which served to activate stakeholder-oriented management. Following these processes, board reform leads to the LTE restriction and PRP introduction, whereas shareholder orientation has no effect on LTE, although it facilitates board reform and promotes PRP introduction. On the other hand, CSR orientation leads to LTE maintenance for regular workers. As a result, the new-J type is led by the combined effects of board reform and CSR orientation, whereas the A-type is led by the combined effects of board reform and shareholder orientation. In this way, we shed light on the diversification of Japanese firms under corporate governance reform.

6. Concluding discussion

We examined the corporate reform undertaken in Japan since around 2000, focusing on corporate governance and the resulting changes in HR practices. First, we found that Japanese firms have preserved their own corporate governance structure despite the increasing shareholder pressure. Contrary to the advocates of the adoption of the US-style shareholder-dominated corporate governance, board reform was not such an overall change (like the US-style committee system) but rather an incremental change within the existing board structure, such as the introduction of an executive officer system. Second, we found that such an incremental change proceeded to a cumulative change in HR practices: particularly the restriction of LTE and introduction of PRP. Third, we found that the notion of the community firm is preserved in the awareness of CSR concerns, and confirmed it as the effect on maintaining LTE as stakeholder orientation. Reform thus proceeds gradually along with both change and continuity. As a result, we found that Japanese firms are diversified into different directions, such as the traditional-J, new-J, A, and declined J types.

Our findings provide empirical support for the arguments of 'gradual institutional change' (Streeck and Thelen 2005, Mahoney and Thelen 2010) and 'evolutionary diversity in the corporate system' (Aoki 2010). In particular, we confirmed that the new-J type, a combination of LTE maintenance and PRP introduction, evolved from traditional Japanese firms through a gradual change under corporate governance reform. However, if only board reform was implemented under shareholder pressure, the A-type, a combination of LTE restriction and PRP introduction, emerges. By contrast, the new-J type, comprised of large, major Japanese firms, is generated by integrating CSR orientation as a proxy of stakeholder orientation into corporate governance reform. In this sense, the new-J type represents not only a hybrid organization composed of LTE and PRP, but also a hybrid structure of corporate governance composed of shareholder and stakeholder orientation.

However, the new-J type is not assured to be maintained indefinitely. If CSR orientation declines and awareness of stakeholder orientation weakens, the new-J type will lose support for its LTE policy. Similarly, if shareholder pressures are more strengthened, and strategic management is intensified by board reform, LTE may be restricted to core workers. Contrariwise, if board reform is attenuated in the new-J type, and the PRP scheme is weakened, then a return to the traditional-J type may occur. Similarly, if CSR orientation declines in the traditional-J type, the declined-J type may appear. In this way, the diversification of Japanese firms will continue. Which type will become dominant depends on corporate performance and on the behaviour of the employees in each type. This will be a topic of future research.

Acknowledgement

I wish to thank two anonymous reviewers for their helpful suggestions.

Disclosure statement

No potential conflict of interest was reported by the author.

Notes

1. In contrast to collective dismissals, there is no internal rule that prescribes individual dismissals. In fact, many disputes occur around individual dismissals.
2. However, the correlation between executive pay and profits disappears when the data are extended from 2002 to 2014. This is likely because executive pay continued the previous level, whereas profits increased more from 2012 to 2014, as shown in Figure 1. It seems that upward trend in executive pay in Japanese firms will be suppressed eventually.

3. It was often said that PRP was introduced with a purpose to reduce labour costs. However, management and unions usually agreed that the total amount of wage payments would not be reduced when PRP was introduced. For instance, the JILPT survey asked about the reason to introduce PRP to 1280 firms in 2004, and 2823 employees in 2005 (JILPT 2007); 77.6 per cent of respondent firms replied 'promoting work motivation', and only 8.4 per cent replied 'reducing labour costs', while 62.4 per cent and 34.8 per cent of employees gave the same answers, respectively. PRP is regarded as a device for promoting motivation by both parties, yet about one-third of employees perceived it as a device for reducing labour costs. This may be because of the curtailment of annual and upgrading wage rises, once perceived as guaranteed. For the sake of reducing labour costs, Japanese firms used non-regular employment instead of using PRP.
4. It is possible to interpret the restriction of LTE to core workers to be a new LTE policy. In this case, LTE policy, both the traditional and new policies, covers almost all Japanese firms. By contrast, we focused on the difference between the two policies because the restricting LTE policy seems to be a step toward the abandoning LTE policy.
5. Hybrid type is not necessarily assured to be stable (Miyamoto and Nohara 2013). As mentioned, when the PRP scheme stresses the short-term performance appraisal, this may conflict with LTE practice. Therefore, the PRP scheme is likely more mitigated in the firm with LTE (hybrid, new-J type) than that without LTE (A-type). We demonstrated that the pay gap is more reduced in the new-J type than the A-type (Miyamoto and Nohara 2013).

References

Ahmadjian, C. L. and Robbins, G., 2005. A clash of capitalisms: Foreign ownership and restructuring in 1990's Japan. *American Sociological Review*, 70 (2), June, 451–471.

Aoki, M., 1988. *Information, incentives and bargaining in the Japanese economy*. Cambridge: Cambridge University Press.

Aoki, M., 1994. Monitoring characteristics of main bank system. *In*: M. Aoki and H. Patrick, eds. *The Japanese main bank system*. Oxford: Oxford University Press, 109–141.

Aoki, M., 2010. *Corporations in evolving diversity*. Oxford: Oxford University Press.

Araki, T., 2005. Corporate governance, labour, and employment relations in Japan: The future of the stakeholder model?. *In*: H. Gospel and A. Pendleton, eds. *Corporate governance and labour management*. Oxford: Oxford University Press.

Brammer, S., Jackson, G., and Matten, D., 2012. Corporate social responsibility and institutional theory: New perspectives on private governance. *Socio-Economic Review*, 10 (1), January, 3–28.

Buchanan, J. and Deakin, S., 2009. In the shadow of corporate governance reform: Change and continuity in managerial practice at listed companies in Japan. *In*: H. Whittaker and S. Deakin, eds. *Corporate governance and managerial reform in Japan*. Oxford: Oxford University Press, 28–69.

Dore, R., 2000. *Stock market capitalism: Welfare capitalism*. Oxford: Oxford University Press.

Dore, R., 2009. Japan's conversion to investor capitalism. *In*: H. Whittaker and S. Deakin, eds. *Corporate governance and managerial reform in Japan*. Oxford: Oxford University Press, 134–162.

Gordon, J. N., 2007. The rise of independent directors in the United States, 1950-2005: Value and stock market prices. *Stanford Law Review*, 59, April, 1465–1568.

Holmstrom, B. and Milgrom P., 1991. Multi-task principal-agent analyses: Incentive contracts, asset ownership, and job design. *Journal of Law, Economics, and Organization*, 7 (special issue), 24–52.

Ishida, M. and Higuchi, J., 2009. *Comparison of human resource management between Japan and the U.S.A.* (in Japanese). Kyoto: Mineruba-shobo.

Jackson, G. and Miyajima, H., 2007. Introduction: The diversity and change of corporate governance in Japan. *In*: M. Aoki, G. Jackson, and H. Miyajima, eds. *Corporate governance in Japan*. Oxford, New York: Oxford University Press, 1–47.

Jacoby, S., 2005. *The embedded corporation: Corporate governance and employment relations in Japan and the United States*. Princeton, N.J.: Princeton University Press.

Japan Association of Corporate Directors, 2016. Survey of the corporate governance in the TSE listed companies (in Japanese). Tokyo: Japan Association of Corporate Governance.

JILPT, 2007. *Firm and employment in Japan* (in Japanese). Tokyo: Japan Institute for Labour Policy and Training.

Kambayashi, R. and Kato, T., 2012. Trend in long-term employment and job security in Japan and the United States: The last twenty-five years. *Working Paper Series, No. 302*, New York: Center on Japanese Economy and Business, Columbia University.

Kato, T., 2001. The end of lifetime employment in Japan?: Evidence from National Surveys and field research. *Journal of the Japanese and International Economies*, 15 (4), 489–514.

Kato, T. and Morishima, M., 2002. The productivity effects of participatory employment practices: Evidence from New Japanese Panel Data. *Industrial Relations*, 41 (4), 487–520.

Kinderman, K., 2012. Free Us Up So We Can Be Responsible: The co-evolution of corporate social responsibility and neo-liberalism in the UK, 1977–2010. *Socio-Economic Review*, 10 (1), January, 29–57.

Koike, K., 1988. *Understanding industrial relations in modern japan* / translated by Mari Sako. London: Macmillan Press.

Kubo, K., 2010. *Corporate governance*. Tokyo: Nihonkeizai-shinbunsya (in Japanese)

Kubo, K., 2011. Dividend policy and employment adjustment. *In*: H. Miyajima, ed. *Japanese corporate governance* (in Japanese). Tokyo: Toyokeizai-shinposya, 409–438.

Mahoney, J. and Thelen, K., 2010. *Explaining institutional change: Ambiguity, agency, and power*. Cambridge: Cambridge University Press.

Marsden, D., 1999. *A theory of employment system: Micro-Foundations of societal diversity*. Oxford: Oxford University Press.

Marsden, D., 2009. The paradox of performance related pay system: Why do we keep adopting them in the face of evidence that they fail to motivate?. *CEP Discussion Papers*, London: No. 946, Centre for Economic Performance, London School of Economics and Political Science.

Matsuura, K., 2001. Relationship between employment reduction and dividend reduction (in Japanese). *Financial Review*, 60, 106–138.

Mayer, C., 2013. *Firm commitment*. Oxford: Oxford University Press.

Miyamoto, M., 2016. Diversification of Japanese firms: How hybrid organizations evolved through corporate governance reform. *Evolutionary and Institutionary Economic Review*, 13 (1), 121–149.

Miyamoto, M. and Nohara, A., 2013. Can hybrid organizations – based on the combination of long-term employment and performance-related pay – operate effectively in Japan?. *Evolutionary and Institutionary Economic Review*, 10 (2), 217–243.

Morishima, M., 1999. The effects of performance pay on the workplace. *Journal of Japan Labor Studies*, 472, 2–14.

Noguchi, Y., 1995. *The 1940 regime* (in Japanese). Tokyo: Toyokeizai-Shiposha.

Olcott, G., 2009. *Conflict and change: Foreign ownership and the Japanese firm*. Cambridge: Cambridge University Press.

Roe, M., 1994. *Strong managers weak owners: The political roots of American finance*. Princeton, N.J.: Princeton University Press.

Rousseau, D., 1995. Psychological contract in organization: Understanding written and unwritten agreements. London: Sage Publication.

Streeck, W. and Thelen, K., 2005. Introduction: Institutional change in advanced political economies. *In*: W. Streeck and K. Thelen, eds. *Beyond continuity*. Oxford: Oxford University Press, 1–39.

Thelen, K., 2009. Institutional change in advanced political economies. *British Journal of Industrial Relations*, 47 (3), 471–498.

Tirole, J., 2001. Corporate Governance. *Econometrica*, 69 (3), 1–35.

Tokyo Stock Exchange, 2013. *White paper on corporate governance* (in Japanese). Tokyo: Tokyo Stock Exchange.

Tokyo Stock Exchange, 2016. *Survey of the nomination of independent directors in Tokyo Stock Exchange* (in Japanese). Tokyo: Tokyo Stock Exchange.

Tsuru, T., Abe, M., and Kubo K., 2005. *Human resource management reform in Japanese firms* (in Japanese). Tokyo: Toyokeizai-Shiposha.

Whittaker, H. and Deakin, S., eds., 2009. *Corporate governance and managerial reform in Japan*. Oxford: Oxford University Press.

Yashiro, N., 2009. *Economics for reforming labor markets* (in Japanese). Tokyo: Toyokeizai-Shiposha.

Yoshimori, K., 1997. *Japanese management and Western management* (in Japanese). Tokyo: Hoso-daigaku-kyouikusinkokai.

Shareholding characteristics and imperfect coverage of the Stewardship Code in Japan

RYOHEI NAKAGAWA

Abstract: While the degree of cross shareholding among corporations, or between banks and companies (referred to as 'insiders' in this article) has been declining since the 1990s, the percentage of shareholding by institutional investors ('outsiders'), or financial intermediaries, has been increasing in Japan. Studies show that both companies and investors are becoming more short-term oriented and are showing herd behaviour. With such a collective mentality, company–investor relations in Japan have experienced a vicious cycle and have thus lowered the market's rate of return. Meanwhile, conventional 'insiders' tend to hold shares in the longer-term, but lack engagement in investee companies' corporate governance. Japan's Stewardship Code requests fund managers 'engage' more than ever in the governance of investees so that investor-company relations become longer-term and the risk of investors' 'exit' decreases. However, the Code only covers the behaviours of 'outsiders' but not those of 'insiders', who still play certain roles among all shareholders. Due to its imperfect coverage, the expected effect of Japan's Stewardship Code in achieving stronger 'engagement' by investors should be limited. To cope with this issue, this article outlines a suggestion that a comprehensive rule covering all types of shareholders should be implemented in Japan.

Introduction

Antinomies of corporate behaviours in Japan

Particularly after the collapse of the bubble economy in the early 1990s, companies in Japan have struggled to slim down their balance sheets, either selling off their assets and repaying their debts, or by seeking short-term profits. These actions were taken collectively, creating a fallacy of composition on the macro scale, and caused a slip into a vicious cycle of low growth and deflation

(Nakagawa 2013, pp. 206–212). Such behaviour can be found not only in corporations but also in institutional investors (Nakagawa 2014, pp. 130–131). Since the early 1990s, the percentage of 'outsider' investors (namely, investors without business affiliations or financial relations to the company being invested in) has been increasing relative to 'insiders' (namely, investors with business affiliations or financial relations) (Franks et al. 2014, p. 2592). On the other hand, various factors during the period, including advancements in information technology, the Asian Crisis, the tech bubble and its bursting, and the subprime bubble and it bursting, have caused higher market volatility, which also induced shorter-term investments. Under such circumstances, investors were losing incentives to hold shares for the longer-run and to 'engage' in corporate governance of investee companies. As such, '(t)he Competitiveness and Incentives for Sustainable Growth: Building Favourable Relationships between Companies and Investors' project, administered by Japan's Ministry of Economy, Trade and Industry (METI) released the Ito Review in August 2014 and also posed concern that 'low profitability of Japanese companies has led to short-termism in company management' (Ministry of Economy, Trade and Industry 2014, p. 13). Companies and financial institutions have been criticised for their self-centred motives at the time of crises in the 1990s and 2000s, even though decisions to 'exit' their investments were rational choices at the micro level.

When an investee company is exposed to a certain downward risk, an investor has an option either to 'voice' or 'exit': to 'voice', in this case, is to engage actively in the investee company's governance issues, and to 'exit' is to divest themselves of their investment. Table 1 (Suto et al., 2005, pp. 20–22) shows the result from questionnaires sent to fund managers in Japan, Germany and the United States.[1] In contrast to widely held perceptions, it indicates that investment periods by Japanese investors tend to be shorter than German and American ones, and such investors are apt to accommodate themselves to public opinion, or take on herd behaviour, relative to foreign investors. As such, both corporate management and investment gradually became shorter-term oriented in the post-bubble period in Japan, inducing volatile market conditions through collective behaviour.

As companies and investors were becoming more short-term oriented, governance transparency was one of the key elements in corporate reforms during the 1990s in Japan. This was particularly due to the Japan–US trade and economic negotiations that highlighted transparency and disclosure from 1989 to 2000, when '[a] key emphasis of the debates was convergence, with the U.S. Government's recommendations to the Japanese Government implying Japan's shift from its established Japanese corporate governance system towards the Anglo-American model' underlining shareholders' ownership of companies (Yonekura et al. 2012, pp. 318–319). America's business interests were concerned with cross-shareholding among companies and commercial banks in Japan, as it was considered to be something shutting out outsiders' entry into the market (Nakagawa 2013, p. 206).

Table 1 Comparison of investment periods and herd behaviour

	Time horizon (% of respondents)		
	Japan	Germany	USA
Days	6.7%	0.8%	2.0%
Weeks	16.8%	13.2%	0.7%
2–6 months	49.2%	59.3%	20.8%
6–12 months	19.1%	21.3%	38.9%
Years	8.2%	5.4%	37.6%
Total	100.0%	100.0%	100.0%
	'I generally follow the trend' (% of respondents)		
1 – Complete approval	2.3%	2.3%	1.4%
2	27.2%	13.5%	4.1%
3	32.8%	34.4%	15.5%
4	17.3%	24.3%	27.0%
5	15.3%	17.0%	35.1%
6 – Completely opposed	5.2%	8.5%	16.9%
Total	100.0%	100.0%	100.0%
Mean	3.320	3.656	4.412

Source: Suto, Menkhoff and Beckmann (2005, pp. 20, 22).

The objective of Japan's Stewardship Code

Under such conditions, Japan's Stewardship Code was introduced in February 2014 by redefining the societal roles of investors. It aims to introduce better corporate governance through investors' longer-term engagement in investee companies' governance.

Investors in general have affirmative attitudes toward the stable development of capital markets. Moreover, they are increasingly expected to engage in investee companies' corporate governance and, thereby, invest longer-term, just as was the case with the Kay Review in the UK, so that the economy as a whole can also avoid market failures (Kay 2013, pp. 16–18). Such movement toward establishing a 'checks-and-balances' function is gradually spreading around the world, and Japan is no exception. In line with the government's economic growth policies, the principle of a Japanese version of a stewardship code was formulated in February 2014. As an objective, it:

> refers to the responsibilities of institutional investors to enhance the *medium- to long-term investment* return for their clients and beneficiaries by improving and fostering the investee companies' corporate values and sustainable growth through constructive engagement, or purposeful dialogue, based on in-depth knowledge of the companies and their business environment. (Financial Services Agency (Japan) 2014, p. 2, emphasis added)

Additionally, as discussed in Nakagawa (2014, p. 133), investors' stewardship should also be institutionalised in tandem with companies' integrated reports so that information-sharing can become mutual and both companies and investors can operate on a level playing field.

Investors have two options when the investee company faces a problem: they can either 'voice' their concerns and commit to the company's reforms, or they can 'exit' (divest) from investing into the company. Particularly after the 1990s, investors chose to 'exit' rather than to 'voice' when companies were going through difficulties. The imbalance of power between investors and companies has been significant, since shareholders always have an option to 'exit' regardless of their will to 'engage'. Such investor behaviours could create a fallacy of composition and the Japanese economy as a whole could lose its capacity to grow. 'Exits' may also happen on a mass scale at the same time, certainly impacting asset prices. Although investors' right to 'exit' should be protected, the Stewardship Code expects fund managers to 'voice' their commitments to investee companies as long as they are investing, and to disclose information about their 'engagement'.

The introduction of the stewardship code can, therefore, be considered an attempt to internalise the information disclosure of investors' engagement (or rational reasons of non-engagement) into the market mechanism without removing the right to 'exit'. Internalisation of externalities in this case is, in other words, to create balanced mutual relations between investors and companies by imposing more transparency on investors, while at the same time allowing their voices to be reflected in investee companies' governance.[2]

The Financial Services Agency in Japan expects investors to:

> A) publicly disclose on their website their intention to accept the Code and information that are required to be disclosed by the principles of the Code, including the policy on how they fulfil the stewardship responsibilities and, if they do not comply with some of the principles, an explanation of the reason; B) annually review and update the disclosed information; and C) notify the Financial Services Agency of the address of their website (the URL) used to disclose the information above. (Financial Services Agency (Japan) 2014, p. 4)

By introducing diverse shareholders' voices, companies are expected to enjoy long-term business improvements and rising share values. According to empirical studies in Japan, companies with increasing ratios, and cases, of exercising voting rights by institutional and foreign shareholders, have shown a tendency to experience better business performances (Miyajima and Yasuda 2012, p. 2). On the other hand, an analysis in Inoue and Ikeda (2010, pp. 11–12) concluded that 'engagements' by aggressive investment funds have increased investee companies' profits and their dividend payments, while proposals through 'engagements' were almost never adopted. Many companies are voicing concerns over such types of investors. Yet Ueda (2014, p. 14) postulates that such aggressive investors are the minority, are not signatories of stewardship codes, and that most major institutional investors are cooperative and compliant. Therefore, this article supports the argument that diverse shareholders' voices would create a positive impact on corporate values.

While diversity is a key to success in Japan's Stewardship Code, not all institutional investors have an interest in complying (Roach 2011, p. 475). Questions remain as to passive funds' engagement. Passive funds only hold minority shares and make decisions based on formal requirements of the investee's targets. Once Japan's Stewardship Code becomes fully institutionalised, however, both active and passive funds will need to comply with their responsibilities as investors. The UNEP Finance Initiative – Principles for Responsible Investment (PRI) also refers to the need for passive funds to be 'consistent with their fiduciary duty and goals of delivering long-term returns to their clients' (UNEP Finance Initiative, Principles for Responsible Investment (PRI) 2011, pp. 4–5).[3] For example, Soda and Mitsusada (2014, pp. 36–39) encourage 'collective engagement' so that they can also play a part within the system in order for many passive investors to comply.

After the formulation of Japan's Stewardship Code in February 2014, fund managers were requested to engage proactively in the governance of investee companies so that the relationship between investors and companies could become longer-term and the risk of investor 'exits' could come under control. By doing so, Japanese companies and investors are expected to dodge short-termism and the fallacy of composition, leading to higher corporate values and stable economic growth. In that sense, stewardship is often considered to represent investors' social responsibility.

Japan's Stewardship Code also embraces some other fundamental issues. The Code adheres to the 'comply or explain' principle and is not a law nor a legally binding regulation (Council of Experts Concerning the Japanese Version of the Stewardship Code, 2013, pp. 3–4). The 'comply or explain' principle was first introduced in the Cadbury Report in 1992 in the UK, and then became the basis of corporate governance in that country. It applies to the market flexibly by not legally forcing investors to comply but by encouraging the market to monitor investor behaviour. Even if fund managers fail to state on their website about stewardship, they face no sanctions, just as with the UK Stewardship Code (Roach 2011, p. 475). However, not all investors are entirely convinced by the 'comply or explain' principle without any coercive power and punitive clause.

Information transparency is also vital. 'Engagement' based on investor stewardship does not simply guarantee an improvement in the quality of the market. For example, in a case of exercising a voting right, fund managers should disclose information appropriately so that recipients can be aware of it. Offering a one-way flow of information is insufficient to sustain the stewardship system. Building a simple structure for an information sharing platform is key.

Additionally, some institutional investors consider that Japan's Stewardship Code is a new sort of corporate social responsibility and cast doubt about the effectiveness of complying with it.[4] It would take time to become widely accepted. Promotional campaigns are also necessary for truly effective enforcement.

Moreover, the Stewardship Code, literally speaking, stipulates the fiduciary duty of fund managers and does not cover any other types of shareholders. The Code, therefore, limits the penetration of its philosophy to all types of shareholders. While Japan's Corporate Governance Code, applied in June 2015, was expected to supplement the coverage of the Stewardship Code from the companies' side, it does not stipulate behaviours of investors (Tokyo Stock Exchange, Inc. 2015, p. 4). Shareholdings by 'insiders', therefore, became a missing piece within monitoring stable and forward-looking investor–company relations.

The transition of shareholder characteristics in Japan

Figure 1 and Table 2 exhibit the transition of the shareholding structure by 'insiders' and 'outsiders'. 'Insiders' in these charts are the shareholders whose primary objectives are not necessarily in maximising investment returns but in maintaining long-term relationships with investee entities. This definition of 'insiders' relies on the criteria of Miyajima and Nitta (2011, p. 109), namely; banks, life and non-life insurance companies, other financial institutions and business corporations. On the other hand, 'outsiders' are those who prioritise

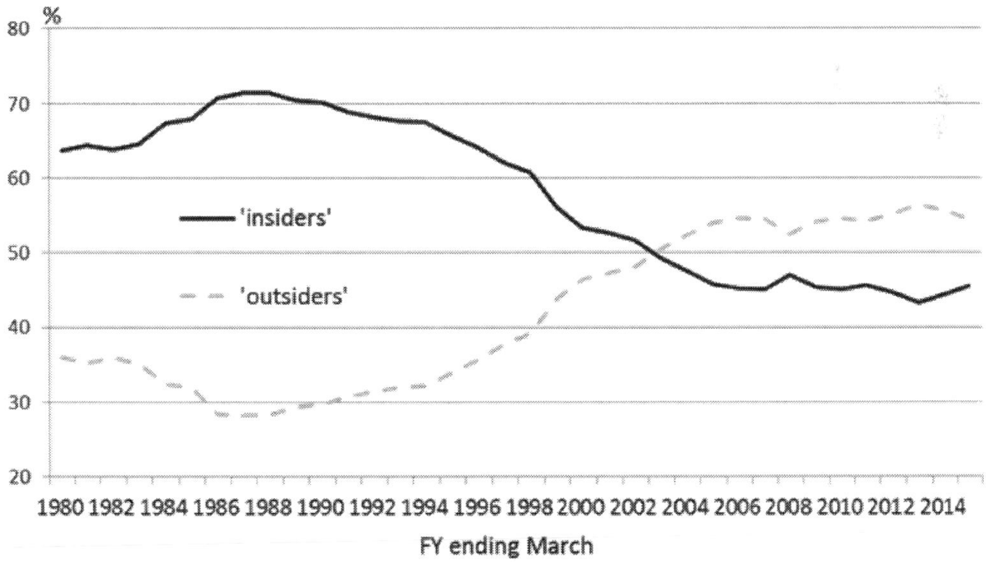

Figure 1 Transition in shareholding ratio by investor category (on a value basis) (1980–2014).
Source: Tokyo Stock Exchange, Kabushiki Bunpu Jokyo Chosa (Survey Data on Distribution of Shares).
Note: Includes JASDAQ-listed companies from FY 2004.

Table 2 Transition in shareholding ratio by investor category, broken-down (on a value basis) (1980–2015)

	Insiders				Outsiders			
Fiscal year ending March	Banks & Trust Banks (less investment and annuity trusts)	Insurance cos. (life & non-life)	Other financial Inst.	Business Corp.	Foreign	Investment Trusts held by banks & trust banks	Annuity Trusts held by banks & trust banks	Individuals
1980	17.6	16.1	3.8	26.2	5.8	1.9	0.4	27.9
1985	18.4	16.4	4.3	28.8	7.0	1.7	0.8	22.3
1990	20.9	15.9	3.3	30.1	4.7	3.7	0.9	20.4
1995	21.4	14.7	2.4	27.2	10.5	2.2	1.8	19.5
2000	19.2	10.9	1.4	21.8	18.8	2.8	5.5	19.4
2005	14.9	7.2	2.4	21.3	26.3	4.3	3.5	19.9
2010	14.7	6.4	2.8	21.2	26.7	4.4	3.2	20.3
2015	15.4	4.7	2.8	22.6	29.8	5.6	1.5	17.5
Peak	21.9 (1996)	16.8 (1986)	4.9 (1987)	30.3 (1987)	31.7 (2014)	5.6 (2015)	6.0 (2001)	27.9 (1980)
Bottom	13.7 (2007)	4.7 (2015)	1.4 (1998, 2000, 2001)	20.8 (2006)	4.1 (1987)	1.4 (1998)	0.4 (1980–82)	17.3 (2014)

Source: Tokyo Stock Exchange, Kabushiki Bunpu Jokyo Chosa (Survey Data on Distribution of Shares).
Note: Includes JASDAQ-listed companies from FY 2004.

maximising investment returns and represent the sum of non-Japanese investment funds held by banks and trust banks, annuity trusts held by banks and trust banks, and individuals.

According to Miyajima and Nitta (2011), the period between the 1970s and the bubble period in the late 1980s was a time when insiders stably played significant roles as shareholders. Even from the mid-1980s, when many large companies raised funds directly from capital markets and started to reduce cross-shareholdings with their 'main banks', the amount was offset by acquisition of shares by financial institutions. These financial institutions purchased massive amounts of financial assets during the bubble period, and the ratio of 'insiders' as a whole was therefore maintained.

In the early 1990s, shares held by foreign investors started to increase in accordance with globalising business and financial activities. The ratio of foreign shareholders shifted from 4.2 per cent in March 1990 to 8.1 per cent in March 1995, and to 18.6 per cent in March 2000. Starting around this period, foreign investors were making significant impacts on stock prices. Being acknowledged by foreign investors, therefore, became strategically important for Japanese companies. In addition, large companies with high international penetration, such as Canon and Sony, gradually reduced their reliance on banks in Japan and increased investment receipts from foreign investors (Miyajima and Nitta 2011, pp. 108–118).

It was mostly the 1997–1998 banking crisis in Japan that made a big impact on the shift from 'insider' shareholding to 'outsiders'. In particular, banks released their shares after the crisis in fear of unrealised losses, followed by companies releasing their bank shares. Banks also rushed to sell off shares after the market price accounting system was introduced in March 2002 in Japan (Miyajima and Nitta 2011, pp. 108–118). Cross-shareholdings by companies were stable most of the time in the 1990s and 2000s. While non-Japanese have consistently increased their presence in Japan's stock market, some domestic companies that were under threat of acquisition increased 'insider' cross-holdings by forming protective alliances in the 2000s. Such instances include the cross-shareholdings among Nippon Steel, Sumitomo Metal Industries and Kobe Steel in Spring 2005, as well as Toyota Motor and Matsushita Electric (now Panasonic) in Spring 2007.

Those companies who increased cross-holdings after the financial crisis around 2008 experienced capital losses, and some of them even needed to book impairment losses. While being delisted from institutional investors' targets, there is still a decent amount of companies continuing to rely on 'insider' cross-shareholdings. As banks are gradually putting off their engagement as lenders, such 'insider' cross-holders are now becoming rarer in corporate governance in Japan (Miyajima and Nitta 2011, pp. 146–147).

While this article defines cross-shareholdings among *keiretsu* companies and between banks and companies as unique to Japan, such types of transactions can also be found outside of Japan. Examples include bank-company cross-holdings in Germany. Additionally, cross-holdings among companies is a common practice all around the world. In that sense, this article does not intend to confine cross-holding behaviours that lack the motive to maximise investment returns only to Japan. Rather, the analysis may also have certain policy implications for countries other than Japan.

Analytical framework

Japan's Stewardship Code currently applies only to fund managers and investment advisors in institutional investors and does not include non-financial business corporations. Corporations, however, have been playing important roles among shareholders in Japan. In addition, the attitudes of banks (and insurance companies) as cross-shareholders are different from when they function as institutional investors. While fund managers fundamentally seek investment returns, the priority of cross-shareholders is often to maintain relations with their counterparts. This article questions whether Japan's Stewardship Code alone is sufficient to achieve its own goal of better corporate governance by not putting 'insiders' within its scope, given the significance of unique relations between companies and shareholders in the country.

The following hypothesis will be investigated in this article: Japan's Stewardship Code may lose substance if 'insider' cross-holdings (as categorised in the previous section) continue to play significant roles in Japan's company–investor relations. This is because shareholdings by 'insiders' are not always based on the motive of maximising investment returns and 'insiders' lack incentives to 'engage' in corporate governance.

The analysis was conducted under a provisional assumption that not only institutional investors but also other institutions, such as banks and business corporations, are to be included within the scope of Japan's Stewardship Codes, given the continuing significance of 'insider' shareholdings. As noted in '[t]he transition of shareholder characteristics in Japan' section, Japan's Stewardship Code will not work effectively to create healthy market conditions between investors and investees if any policy measures to monitor shareholdings by 'insiders' are not implemented at the same time.

To investigate the hypothesis above, the expected effects of Japan's Stewardship Code are portrayed in a matrix in order to explore whether they are effective and what effects are not. The following types of shareholders in Japan were investigated in this process:

- 'Outsiders', namely investors without existing business affiliations or financial relations (foreign investors, investment trusts held by banks and trust banks, annuity trusts held by banks and trust banks, and individuals);
- 'Insiders', namely investors with business affiliations or financial relations (banks, insurance companies, other financial institutions and business corporations).

Table 3 Analytical overview

	Before the 1990s	After the 1990s	Expected effects by Japan's Stewardship Code
Shareholding market condition	• Long-term cross shareholding • Among keiretsu companies • Bank-company	• Mix of 'insiders' and 'outsiders' • Volatile: frequent 'exits'	• Mix of 'insiders' and 'outsiders' • Less volatility due to less frequent 'exits'
Corporate governance characteristics	• In-house governance • By 'insiders', particularly by 'main banks' • Infrequent 'voices'	• In transition: Increasing external board members, decreasing 'main bank' involvements • More 'exits' than 'voices'	• Limited improvement: Stronger 'voices' from 'outsiders', while 'insiders' still lack incentives to 'voice'
'Outsiders'	• Minority • Infrequent 'voices' • Profit motive	• Increasing • Frequent 'exits' rather than 'voices' • Profit motive	• Effective impact by the Code • The Code's direct target • Profit motive
'Insiders'	• Majority • Minimal 'voices' • Prioritise relationship	• Decreasing • Minimal 'voices' • Prioritise relationship	• Minimal impact • Coverage loophole of the Code • Still lack incentives to 'voice' • Prioritise relationship

These two types of investors, as well as shareholding market conditions and corporate governance characteristics, are arranged vertically in Table 3, while the following three chronological eras are arranged horizontally: before the 1990s, after the 1990s, and expected and desired effects of Japan's Stewardship Code.

This paper regards 'the 1990s' as the turning point of Japan's corporate governance and shareholding structure, and the following articles back up this position with ample reasoning. Miyajima and Nitta (2011, pp. 112–113) define 1990–1996 as a period of a sharp increase in the number of foreign shareholders, and 1997–2004 as a period of cross-shareholding dissolution in Japan. Moreover, Ota 2014 describes that the Japanese style of corporate governance, such as cross-shareholding, the 'main bank' system, and the internal promotion of board members, has also shifted drastically since the asset bubble collapse around the 1990s (Ota 2014, p. 43).

An effectual analysis is provided in each cell in Table 3 based on the literature. As a conclusion, the Code's hypothetical impacts on 'outsider' and 'insider' shareholders is described. Drawing upon the lessons learned from the investigation, a policy recommendation for achieving an effective investor–company relations is presented at the end.

While relying on existing analyses of the transition of Japan's shareholding structures and corporate governance, such as that of Miyajima and Nitta (2011), this article attempts to provide its own view on the impacts between Japan's Stewardship Codes and cross-shareholdings.

Arsalidou (2012, pp. 417–418) harbours reservations about the necessity of stewardship, as most of the literature surrounding stewardship is based on the rational choice model of institutional investors, while the findings of behavioural economics cast doubt on such rational choices. In contrast, this article adopts a stance that the implementation of the stewardship code is an attempt to internalise the negative externalities, or, in other words, to coordinate the behaviours of companies and investors closer to such rational choices within the system of the market economy.

For the case of Japan's Stewardship Code, it is difficult to fit everything inside the rational choice model, because it does not cover the 'insider' cross-shareholders that are not motivated to maximise investment returns. This article attempts to demonstrate the loophole of Japan's Stewardship Code and its impacts on investor-company relations.

Expected effects of Japan's Stewardship Code

With regards to 'outsiders', Japan's Stewardship Code directly targets them and will have an effective impact on their behaviour. Shareholding by 'outsiders' is profit-driven in the first place. Japan's Stewardship Code fundamentally covers fund managers' fiduciary duty, because 'outsiders' (namely foreign investors, investment trusts held by banks and trust banks, annuity trusts held by banks and trust banks, and individuals investing through fund managers) are the direct targets, and should work effectively by engaging in corporate governance of the investees.

Another important effect is that institutional investors will move away from being speculative by setting proper objectives and conducting thorough research about the target companies. Having such an effect is the whole intention of deploying the stewardship rules. Additionally, Japan's Corporate Governance Code only focuses on investee companies' points of view and does not monitor the behaviours of 'insider' shareholders.

Regarding the behaviour of 'insiders', they should also be monitored, as many of them lack the motivation to 'voice'. Motivation of shareholding 'insiders' is a missing piece within the series of corporate governance reforms in so-called Abenomics, namely enacting Japan's Stewardship and Corporate Governance Codes, as well as encouraging companies to release integrated annual reports.

The motive of shareholding by 'insiders' weighs heavily on maintaining relationships and is often different from that of maximising foreseeable returns. For example, cross-shareholdings among *keiretsu* companies that share group identities and 'main banks' that have a legacy of long-term relations with their borrowers, do not place profit maximisation as a top priority.

A noteworthy case includes that of Mitsubishi Motors Corporation, when the company was facing a risk of collapse after it covered-up recall incidents in 2000 and 2004. As Daimler-Chrysler abandoned the idea of a capital alliance and no other domestic or foreign automakers bid to rescue Mitsubishi Motors, the 'big three' of the Mitsubishi Group, namely Mitsubishi Heavy Industry, Mitsubishi Corporation, and Bank of Tokyo-Mitsubishi, decided to rescue it by holding newly issued preference stocks. In this case, these 'big three' did not have the intention to maximise their investment returns. It was done purely to support their desperate sworn ally (Toyokeizai Online 2013). Such an alliance implies that the notion of maximising returns is limited. Yet this relationship is currently changing, as Nissan decided to acquire a 34 per cent stake in Mitsubishi Motors in May 2016, a day after the other Mitsubishi companies finally abandoned it following another cover-up scandal.

Throughout the 2000s, the alleged decrease in horizontal *keiretsu* cross-holdings was not significant and saw only small fluctuations, as such cross-holdings aimed to protect themselves from hostile takeovers (Miyajima and Nitta 2011, p. 121). This meant that 'insider' shareholdings are still significant and cannot be ignored.

As for bank-company relations, cross-shareholding has been a symbol of a commitment to long-term banking relations in Japan. This type of cross-holding is a legacy from the post-Second World War banking system. Since the immediate post-Second World War period, banks held their borrowers' shares by swapping piles of loans for equities. As a 'main bank', engagement in the borrowers' corporate governance is considered one of the core responsibilities, regardless of adhering to stewardship codes. Such behaviour becomes noticeable when borrowers' businesses are facing difficulties, since many Japanese bankers are proud of supporting their counterparts in need. Yet banks' commitments are shifting from a monitoring mode to those of risk-hedging and/or simply providing financial services (Hirota 2009, pp. 20–21), although conventional bank–company relations are still common. In addition, their engagement can become weaker if the amount of lending also decreases.

In contrast to the above trend, borrowers are unlikely to engage in the lenders' governance regardless of the Code's institutionalisation. There are few or no cases of companies stepping into the governance of their 'main banks' in modern Japan.

'Insiders' still hold a significant percentage of shares, at over 40 per cent as of 2015 according to Figure 1, representing the fact that Japan's Stewardship Code has a crucial loophole in only covering fund managers' fiduciary duty and not 'insider' shareholdings.

Conclusion

In light of the fact that investor behaviour is not necessarily based on rational choices, the analysis in the previous sections was conducted on the basis that the institutionalisation of Japan's Stewardship Code is a process of creating a platform for making non-rational investment decisions into relatively more rational ones.

In reality, however, the Code is not expected to make a drastic change in shifting Japan's corporate governance to a more transparent and market-oriented one. This article has shed light on the fact that one of the reasons the philosophy of investor stewardship will not permeate to widespread parts of Japan's business and investment communities lies in its loophole of not covering 'insider' shareholding. Additionally, Japan's Corporate Governance Code only focuses on investee companies' points of view and does not monitor the behaviours of 'insider' shareholders. Therefore, the status quo of Japan's Stewardship Code could lose substance.

The philosophy and the conceptual framework of Japan's Stewardship Code is sublime and ideal. Business, financial, investment, legal and regulatory communities in the country should further discuss and move toward the true success of this ongoing initiative. At the same time, on the policy side, various measures from different angles to improve the country's corporate governance should be formulated and implemented. Moreover, the institutionalisation of the Stewardship Code should be planned and enforced in tandem with reform of corporate information disclosures, namely integrated reports, as Nakagawa (2014, pp. 133–134) emphasised. Investor stewardship, integrated reports, and good corporate governance are an inseparable trio: lacking any one of them will not make corporate-investor relations more sustainable, instead the economy will revert back to its previous state of highly volatile and vulnerable economy. Yet with the abovementioned set of policies, monitoring of shareholding 'insiders' is still missing. The government is encouraged to set up a policy to encourage more purposeful dialogue between company managers and their 'insider' shareholders. Such reforms may pave the way for fostering the investee companies' corporate values.

Acknowledgements

The author would like to thank Thomas W. French for his constructive comments that contributed to improving the final version of the paper. He would also like to thank the editors for their generous comments during the review process.

Disclosure statement

No potential conflict of interest was reported by the author.

Notes

1. According to Suto et al. (2005, pp. 10–11) surveys on investment behaviour and information processing were conducted in parallel in the three countries, using an identical format during the period between April 2003 and February 2004: Japan – 488 valid responses from trust banks, life insurers, and investment advisory companies; Germany – 263 valid responses from investment trust fund companies; and United States – 148 valid responses from fund managers.
2. There is also a Platform of Responsible Investment (PRI) Clearinghouse that aims: 'for collaborative engagement initiatives. It provides PRI signatories with a private forum to pool resources, share information, enhance influence and engage with companies, stakeholders, policymakers and other actors in the investment value chain on environmental, social and corporate governance issues across different sectors and regions' (PRI Association 2015). There are 469 signatories involved, 1661 companies contacted, and 589 posts by the clearinghouse, as of 18 January 2015.
3. It should be noted that PRI relates to environment, social and governance (ESG) factors and does not necessarily focus on bilateral relations with investee companies.
4. Blomgren (2011, p. 272) conducted a survey of the 15 largest textile companies in Norway and concluded that 'there is no business case for CSR in the sense of helping achieve profits above industry average, but only a business case in the sense of helping achieve profits at industry average'.

Orcid

Ryohei Nakagawa http://orcid.org/0000-0003-1205-1414

References

Arsalidou, D., 2012. Institutional investors, behavioural economics and the concept of stewardship. *Law and Financial Markets Review*, 6 (6), 410–421.

Blomgren, A., 2011. Does corporate social responsibility influence profit margins? A case study of executive perceptions. *Corporate Social Responsibility and Environmental Management*, 18, 263–274.

Council of Experts Concerning the Japanese Version of the Stewardship Code, the, 2013. Principle for responsible institutional investors – Japan's Stewardship Code – to promote sustainable growth of companies through investment and dialogue. Financial Services Agency. 26 December 2013. Available from: http://www.fsa.go.jp/en/refer/councils/stewardship/ [Accessed 12 December 2014].

Financial Services Agency (Japan), 2014. *Draft final report – Principles for responsible institutional investors – Japan's Stewardship Code – To promote sustainable growth of companies through.* The Council of Experts Concerning the Japanese Version of the Stewardship Code investment and dialogue (dated February 26, 2014). Available from: http://www.fsa.go.jp/singi/stewardship/siryou/20140227.html [Accessed 19 March 2014].

Franks, J., Mayer, C. and Miyajima, H., 2014. The ownership of Japanese corporations in the 20th century. *Review of Financial Studies*, 27 (9), 2580–2625, September 2014.

Hirota, S., 2009. Nihon no Main Bank Kankei: Monitaringu kara Risuku Hejji he (Japan's Main Bank Relations: From Monitoring to Risk Hedging). RIETI Discussion Paper Series 09-J-023, August 2009. Tokyo: Research Institute of Economy, Trade & Industry.

Inoue, M. and Ikeda, H., 2010. Nihon no Koporeto Gabanansu to Akutyibisuto Fando no Kankei (Relations between Japan's Corporate Governance and Activist Funds). *Journal of Business Management*, 25, 3–14.

Kay, J., 2013. *The kay review of UK equity markets and long–term decision making – Third report of session 2013–14.* House of Commons – Business, Innovation and Skills Committee. Available from: http://www.parliament.uk/business/committees/committees-a-z/commons-select/business-innovation-and-skills/inquiries/parliament-2010/the-kay-review/ [Accessed 19 January 2014].

Ministry of Economy, Trade and Industry, 2014. *Ito review of competitiveness and incentives for sustainable growth – Building favourable relationships between companies and investors – Final report*, August 2014. Available from: http://www.meti.go.jp/english/press/2014/0806_04.html [Accessed 18 December 2014].

Miyajima, H. and Nitta, K., 2011. *Kabushiki Shoyu Kozo no Tayoka to Sono Kiketsu (Diversification of shareholding structure and its consequences)*; Chapter 2 (pp. 105–149) of *Nihon no Kigyo Tochi (Corporate Governance in Japan)*. Tokyo: Toyo Keizai Shimpo Sha.

Miyajima, H. and Yasuda, T., 2012. Henbo suru Nihon Kigyo no Shoyukozo wo Ikani Rikaisuruka (Understanding the shifting structure of Japan's corporate shareholdings). *Financial Research Centre (FSA Institute) Discussion Paper*; DP2011-11, March 2012, Tokyo.

Nakagawa, R., 2013. A perspective on antinomies of corporate behaviors after the 1990s in Japan. *The Ritsumeikan Journal of International Studies*, 25-3, 203–218.

Nakagawa, R., 2014. Will the institutionalisation of integrated reports in Japan meet the conditions of Coase's theorem? *The Ritsumeikan Journal of International Studies*, 27-1, 129–149.

Ota, T. 2014. Nihonban Suchuwadoshippu ga Kigyo ni Ataeru Eikyo (Influence of Japan's Stewardship Code on Companies). *Security Analysts Journal of Japan*, August 2014, 41–51.

PRI Association, 2015. *Principle for responsible investment – Clearinghouse*. Available from: http://www.unpri.org/areas-of-work/clearinghouse/ [Accessed 18 January 2015].

Roach, L., 2011. The UK Stewardship Code. *Journal of Corporate Law Studies*, 11 (2), 463–493.

Soda, D. and Mitsusada, Y., 2014. Unyogaisha kara mita suchuwadoshippu kodo – seicho senryaku ni shisuru tameni (Stewardship code from the perspective of investors – to contribute to the growth strategy). *Security Analysts Journal of Japan*, August 2014, 29–40.

Suto, M., Menkhoff, L. and Beckmann, D., 2005. Behavioural biases of institutional investors under pressure from customers: Japan and Germany vs the US, *Waseda University Institute of Finance Working Paper Series*; WIF-05-006, November 2005, Tokyo.

Tokyo Stock Exchange, 2015. Japan's corporate governance code: Seeking sustainable corporate growth and increased corporate value over the mid- to long-term, Tokyo Stock Exchange, Inc. Available from: http://www.jpx.co.jp/english/equities/listing/cg/ [Accessed 3 November 2016].

Tokyo Stock Exchange, *Kabushiki bunpu jokyo chosa (Survey data on distribution of shares)*. Available from: http://www.tse.or.jp/market/data/examination/distribute/ [Accessed 18 December 2014].

Toyo Keizai Online, 2013. Mitsubishi jidosha 'kanzen hitoridachi' ni muke nokoru kenen (Concerns left for Mitsubishi Motor's 'independence'). Available from: http://toyokeizai.net/articles/-/23537 [Accessed 8 January 2015].

Ueda, R., 2014. Suchuwadoshippu kodo ga kabunushi sokai ni ataeru eikyo (Impacts of Stewardship Codes on shareholders' meetings), *Shoji Homu (Commercial Law Review)*, Annex No.361, April 2014, 6–13.

UNEP Finance Initiative, Principles for Responsible Investment (PRI), 2011. *Responsible investment in passive management strategies – Case studies and guidance.* dated January 2011. Available from: http://www.unpri.org/areas-of-work/implementation-support/passive-funds/ [Accessed 18 December 2014].

Yonekura, A., Gallhofer, S. and Haslam, J., 2012. Accounting disclosure, corporate governance and the battle for markets: The case of trade negotiations between Japan and the U.S., *Critical Perspectives on Accounting 23*, 2012, 312–331.

'Growth oriented' corporate governance reform – can it solve Japan's performance puzzle?

FRANZ WALDENBERGER

Abstract: Recent governance reforms in Japan aim at promoting 'the establishment of an environment that supports appropriate risk-taking by the senior management.' The article evaluates the reforms on the basis of two questions: do the reforms tackle the right issues? And will they be effective? The Japanese economy faces indeed a performance puzzle. Despite Japan's strong efforts in the field of research and development, its excellent work force and abundant financial capital, the economy is performing poorly in terms of productivity. The performance puzzle seems to be closely related to the way large Japanese companies are governed, namely by boards filled with internally promoted lifetime employees. However, the correlation between board composition and performance is spurious. Both are influenced by a third factor, which manifests itself in the predominance of in-house careers. In-house careers determine the composition of boards and have, over the last twenty years, had a negative impact on economic performance. The governance reforms do not address the root of Japan's performance puzzle. They may nevertheless provide an important stimulus for redesigning the way Japanese corporations recruit, train and promote future leaders.

1. Setting the scene

1.1. Soft rules – strong ambitions

Since the early 1990s, the governance of Japanese corporations listed on the country's stock exchanges has regularly been the subject of reform (Shishido 2001, 2004, 2007). The more recent initiatives, the Japan Stewardship Code (JSC) introduced in 2014 (Council of Experts 2014), the revision of the Companies Act in 2015 (Goto 2013, Nakamura 2015) and the adoption of a Corporate Governance

Code (JGC) (Council of Experts 2015) in the same year differ from previous measures in two respects. First, they represent soft law. The institutional investors addressed by the JSC are encouraged, but not obliged to sign the Code. As indicated by its formal title, the Code contains 'principles for responsible institutional investors' rather than narrowly defined rules, and it applies a 'comply-or-explain' approach allowing signatories to not apply principles, if they state the reasons for not doing so. The Code is therefore not legally binding (JSC par 11). A major new element of the revised Companies Act is the prescription to have at least one independent outside director on the boards of listed companies. It is also based on the 'comply-or-explain' principle giving companies the possibility to deviate. Principle 4.8 of the JGC goes one step further than the revised Companies Act by demanding companies have at least two independent outside directors. Contrary to the JSC, the JGC is binding for companies listed on Japan's major stock exchanges (JGC par 13), but otherwise it offers the same flexibility. It is based on general principles rather than clearly specified rules and also applies the 'comply or explain' approach. The stipulations are not legally binding in the strict sense.

The second common characteristic differentiating the recent reforms from earlier ones is the strongly held expectation that they will enhance corporate performance and economic growth. They play a central role in the 'Japan Revitalization Strategy', which forms the 'growth strategy' or the third arrow' of 'Abenomics'.[1] The 'Japan Revitalization Strategy' updated September 2015 features corporate governance reform as a key policy measure under the revised strategy (Cabinet Office 2015, p. 4). The progress report on 'Abenomics' updated October 2015 mentions the reforms directly under the section 'III. Corporate Earning Power Enhancement' (Government of Japan 2015, p. 6). 'Growth orientation' is explicitly referred to in both Codes. Three of the seven JSC principles mention growth. Principle three asks institutional investors to monitor investee companies with 'an orientation towards the sustainable growth of the companies'. Principle five states that the policy on voting 'should be designed to contribute to the sustainable growth of investee companies'. The seventh principle emphasizes that institutional investors need to make sure they have the appropriate expertise and skill 'to contribute positively to the sustainable growth of their investee companies'. 'Growth-oriented governance' promoting 'healthy corporate entrepreneurship' is stated as a major objective of the JGC (par 7). Principle 4.2 of the Code explicitly emphasizes 'the establishment of an environment that supports appropriate risk-taking by the senior management' as a major role and responsibility of the board.

1.2. Questions addressed

The following analysis will focus on the second characteristic, the explicit growth orientation or – to use the Japanese term – the 'seme no gabanansu' goal of the recent reforms. The concept of 'growth oriented' governance is based on the assumption that large Japanese corporations are suffering from a too risk averse management approach preventing them from putting the resources under their command to their best use.[2] It is further assumed that engaging institutional investors and hiring independent outside directors can contribute to a more risk friendly environment, thus stimulating investment and growth.

The analysis presented below will elaborate on both assumptions. The first assumption is basically an empirical one. Do Japanese companies and in the aggregate the Japanese economy underperform? The question will be addressed in the next subsection and it will be answered in the affirmative. Given Japan's technological potential, the education level and skills of its workforce and the abundant amount of financial capital, Japan seems indeed to be underperforming in terms of productivity.

The assumption that the recent corporate governance reforms will improve economic performance must be judged on three grounds. What possible theoretical channels are there by which the reforms may impact performance? To what extent are these channels empirically relevant in the case of Japan? Can we say that performance actually improved due the reform? The last question can only be answered after a certain time lag to allow the reforms to exert their potential influence on performance. It can therefore not be taken up here. The analysis conducted in the third subsection will instead concentrate on the first two issues. It will be argued that (1) 'seme no gabanansu' differs from the standard theoretical arguments linking corporate governance and economic performance, (2) the assumed link is spurious in the sense that (3) there is a common structural factor that induces the management behaviour targeted by the reforms and which has been hampering performance over the last twenty years. The structural factor is represented by in-house careers that spread and became common practice after the Second World War. In-house careers proved highly successful during Japan's economic catch-up. They are still predominant and continue to represent a core institution of corporate Japan. However, under a changing demographic and economic environment, their constraints on the use and allocation of productive resources have become increasingly exposed. The final subchapter elaborates on the implications of the analysis. It concludes that corporate governance reform will only be effective to the extent that it promotes the creation of inter-firm career opportunities for skilled and managerial labour.

1.3. Contribution to research and policy debate

The article's central argument that the predominance of in-house careers impacts both corporate governance and economic performance is novel in four respects. First, there is an important body of literature associating Japan's employment system with the miraculous growth and structural adjustment from after the war until the early 1990s (Dore 1988, Odagiri 1994). There are also many observers arguing that the system has become outdated and needs to be reformed (Jones and Urasawa 2011, Yashiro 2011, Aoyagi and Ganelli 2013). In fact, labour market reforms form a central part of Abenomics' growth strategy (Government of Japan 2015, p. 11). The analysis presented in this article differs in its emphasis on in-house careers as the core of Japan's employment system. As will be shown, in-house careers are closely related, but in many respects distinct from lifetime employment. In addition, the predominance of in-house careers is a structural characteristic. They are not prescribed by law, but evolved within a specific economic context. They are complemented by other parts of the economic system. The implied path dependency explains their persistence even in an unfavourable economic environment (Aoki 1994, Gilson and Roe 1999).

Second, the article adds both empirically and theoretically to the branch of research that has been trying to explain Japan's cconomic performance over the last two decades (Posen 1998, Koo 2003, OECD 2015a). Empirically, the comparative analysis contrasting resource conditions and performance among nineteen OECD countries offers a new and straightforward approach to evaluating economic performance. Theoretically, the arguments relating the predominance of in-house careers to Japan's underperformance contribute to the strand of research that focuses on structural causes. Japan's past economic performance can, of course, not be explained by a single factor or by structural causes alone. The point made here is that the predominance of in-house careers must not be overlooked when trying to make sense out of Japan's past economic performance.

Third, there is an abundant literature on Japanese corporate governance (Dore 2000, Learmount 2002, Milhaupt and West 2004, Aoki et al 2007, Whittaker and Simon 2009). A large amount of effort has been invested in describing the differences in corporate governance between the Japanese and Western, especially Anglo-Saxon economies in terms of institutions, underlying values, and behavioural outcomes (Aguilera and Jackson 2003, Jackson and Miyajima 2007). The importance of in-house careers as a central pillar of the Japanese system has, however, not been fully appreciated, despite the fact that human resource management has been a central theme in the comparative analysis of the Japanese firm (Aoki and Dore 1994, Imai and Komiya 1994).

Finally, the article is one of the first attempts to evaluate the recent governance reforms. The reforms received much attention in the international press.[3] But there have so far been few contributions trying to clarify and critically assess the assumptions underlying the concept of 'seme no gabanansu'.[4]

2. Japan's performance puzzle

Underperformance means that corporations consistently fail in making best use of the resources they manage. At the aggregate level of an economy, this is equivalent to saying that a country has not been exploiting the full potential of its domestic factors of production such as technology, labour and financial capital. There is of course no theory to tell us what can best be achieved with a certain quantity and quality of resources. We can only argue in relative terms by drawing comparisons with other economies. If, within this group of economies, a country ranks high with regard to its resource conditions, but low in terms of performance, it may be said to be underperforming. We will compare Japan's resource conditions and performance with nineteen OECD countries (see Table A1 in the appendix). The observation period covers. in most cases, the last twenty years to exclude short-term business cycle effects.

Resource conditions are assessed with regard to technology, the educational attainment of the adult population and the availability of cheap financial capital. Performance is depicted by measures that relate to the level and growth of productivity and international presence. The respective indicators, definitions and sources are listed in Table 1.

R1 tells us how much an economy invests to achieve technological advances. If research and development activities are undertaken in an efficient way, a higher ratio indicates broader or faster technological advances and a correspondingly larger pool or higher level of technology. R2 refers to 'patent families'. These are patents based on the same invention applied for at different patent offices. The term 'Triadic patent families' is used for applications in the US, the EU and Japan (Dernis and Khan 2004). Only highly valuable inventions will afford the cost of being protected on a global scale. A higher value of R2 indicates therefore a larger pool of highly valuable technological know-how. R3 is a measure of the educational attainment of an economy's working age population (OECD 2014, p. 40). The higher R3, the better educated an economy's working force. R4 is the availability of long-term capital as reflected by the rate of return on long-term government bonds. The lower R4 the more abundant the supply of domestic funds relative to demand.

Productivity measures the relationship between input and output levels. The main input categories are working hours and capital services. Higher productivity is associated with increases in the quality of factors of production and with technological advances. The labour and capital productivity measures P1 and P2 are based on the services provided for by the persons and the stock of capital employed. For employment, these are the actual hours worked. Measuring the services provided by the employed stock of capital is less straightforward. P2 uses the costs associated with renting capital goods and their depreciation during production to estimate the volume of capital services. The OECD database provides only data on the annual growth rates of capital productivity (OECD 2015b, p. 26). The same is true for multifactor productivity, which measures growth in output that cannot be attributed to increases in total working hours and capital inputs (OECD 2015b, p. 30). P3 is generally associated with improvements in production techniques resulting from technological advances.

Table 1 List of indicators to assess resource conditions and performance.

Definition		Measure	Time period	Source
		(a) Resource conditions		
Technology				
R1	Ratio of gross expenditure on research and development to GDP	Per cent	1994–2013	OECD, Main Science Technology Indicators, OECD.Stat, 18 October 2015
R2	Share in global 'triadic patent family' applications	Per cent	1994–2013	OECD, Main Science Technology Indicators, OECD.Stat, 20 October 2015
Educational attainment of adult population				
R3	Share of population in age group 24–65 with tertiary education	Per cent	2000, 2005–2013	OECD, Education at a Glance Interim Report, 2015, Table 1.4, 24 October 2015
Availability of financial capital				
R4	Long-term interest rate on government bonds adjusted by annual rate of change of consumer price index (all items)	Per cent	1994–2013	OECD, Economic Projections, Economic Outlook No 97 OECD.Stat, 24 October 2015; Key Short-Term Economic Indicators, OECD.Stat, 24 October 2015
		(b) Performance		
Productivity				
P1	GDP per hour worked in current prices and converted in US dollars using current purchasing power parity rates (PPP)	US dollar	1994–2013	OECD, Productivity, Level of GDP per capita and productivity, OECD.Stat, 24 October 2015
P2	Annual growth rate of capital productivity	Per cent	1995–2013	OECD, Productivity, Growth in GDP per capita, productivity and ULC, OECD.Stat, 24 October2015
P3	Annual growth rate of multifactor productivity	Per cent	1995–2013	OECD, Productivity, Growth in GDP per capita, productivity and ULC, OECD.Stat, 24 October 2015
International presence				
P4	Share in world export markets for goods and services	Per cent	1994–2013	UNCTAD, International trade in goods and services, Trade trends, UNCTAD.Stat, 24 October 2015
P5	Share in global stock of outward FDI in per cent	Per cent	1994–2013	UNCTAD, Foreign direct investment, UNCTAD.Stat, 24 October 2015

Table 2 Japan's ranking with regard to resource conditions and performance among nineteen OECD countries; for explanation of indicators and sources see Table 1.

Indicator	Explanation	Rank
Resource conditions		
R1	Average over period 1994 to 2013	3
R2	Average over period 1994 to 2013	1
R3	Average over years 2000, 2005 to 2013/2014	2
R4	Average over period 1994–2013	1
Performance		
P1	Average level over period 1994 to 2013	17
P2	Average growth rate over period 1995 to 2013	17
P3	Average growth rate over period 1995 to 2013	12
P4	Change over period 1994 to 2013	19
P5	Change over period 1994 to 2013	17

International presence reflects the exploitation of comparative advantage and economies of scale. For advanced economies, scale effects resulting from a highly skilled labour force and a broad pool as well as high level of technology tend to be more important than comparative advantage (Ethier 1982). A higher international presence exploits these scale advantages to a larger extent. This should also contribute to higher productivity. International presence and productivity can therefore be seen as mutually re-enforcing (Young 1928). International presence is measured in terms of shares in world exports of goods and services, but also with regard to the share in the global stock of outward foreign direct investment (FDI). Outward FDI is another way to exploit know-how. It may substitute for exports, but it often supports exports as well as international supply chains (Nicoletti et al 2003, pp. 22–23, Hard and Ries 2004, pp. 412–414).

Table 2 gives an overview of Japan's resource conditions and performance, based on the indicators listed in Table 1. As can be seen, Japan ranks among the top three for all four indicators. Japan comes third in its expenditures on R&D relative to GDP and first with regard to international patent applications. In terms of educational attainment it is second after Canada. The high level of education by Japan's working population has recently been corroborated by the first OECD skill survey, which tested the numeracy and literacy proficiency of persons aged 16 to 65 among twenty OECD countries (OECD 2013). In both categories, Japanese respondents performed best.

Japan had on average the lowest real long-term interest rates over the twenty-year period from 1994 to 2013. The period covers the aftermath of Japan's financial crisis that started with the burst of the stock market and real estate bubble in 1990/1992 and cumulated in failures of large financial institutions in 1998. The crisis was only overcome in 2003. Up until the latter half of the 1990s, Japanese corporations suffered from severe balance sheet problems (Koo 2003), which meant that they would not take on additional debt despite historically low interest rates. The corporate sector succeeded in reducing its debt ratio as the government sector took over the role of main borrower. In fact, corporations continued to improve their equity positions, while acquiring more and more cash on the asset side of their balance sheets. As a result, the amount of total investment between 1997 and 2013 remained well below total cash flow, implying that Japan's corporate sector provided the economy with financial capital instead of absorbing savings from private households as standard economic textbooks would suggest.[5] Today, Japan's corporate sector boasts historically high equity and liquidity ratios (Waldenberger 2014, pp. 49–50). The ratio of cash holdings to total assets at listed companies in Japan is twice as large as in other advanced economies (OECD 2015a). The positive side of it is that Japanese companies are today financially very strong. The negative side is that they do not seem to know how to make use of these financial resources. This is exactly what 'seme no gabanansu' wants to change.

Table 2 also shows Japan's performance over the last twenty years with regard to the indicators P1 to P5. In contrast to the comparison of the resource condition, Japan occupies the last three ranks, except for multifactor productivity growth (P3), where it achieves lower middle rank 12. As the third largest national economy Japan naturally occupies a top position in international trade and foreign direct investment. Due to the rise of China, many leading economies have lost export market share over the two decades. However, Japan's loss is twice as large as the average loss of the group. The country performed worst among the nineteen OECD countries in terms of relative change of export market share (P4). The strong loss in export market was not compensated by outward FDI. On the contrary, Japan experienced the third largest relative decline in the share of outward FDI (P5).

Comparing Japan's excellent resource conditions with its clearly less than average performance we indeed confront a puzzle. Japanese corporations seem not to have been able to leverage their large pool and high level of technology, the high educational attainment of their employees and the availability and cheap access to financial capital. The reasons are certainly manifold and complex (OECD 2012, 2015a, Cabinet Office 2015). It is not possible and also not the purpose of this article to provide a comprehensive analysis of the performance puzzle. Instead we will focus on the possible role of corporate governance. The recent reforms assume that corporate governance can at least partly be blamed for Japan's disappointing performance.

3. In-house careers – the link between governance and performance

3.1. *In search for the logic underlying 'seme no gabanansu'*

The corporate governance of a corporation determines how top management is directed and controlled, to whom it is responsible, how it is appointed, rewarded and dismissed (Committee 1992). Core governance institutions are the board of directors, ownership structures, shareholder rights including rules pertaining to shareholder meetings, takeover regulations, disclosure rules and executive remuneration packages (OECD 2004, pp. 11–12). Governance becomes especially important for companies that are run by employed managers, which is typically the case for listed companies. By protecting outside investors, sound corporate governance ensures the functioning of stock markets. Stock markets in turn are important for two reasons. They allow companies to raise additional equity capital to finance new risky investment and they provide investors with liquidity and the ability to diversify risk through the trading of listed stock. Sound corporate governance thus indirectly contributes to growth and innovation. Corporate governance reform has always been justified along these lines of argument (Hermalin and Weisbach 2006). Correspondingly, reform efforts tended to focus on improving the monitoring function of boards, strengthening the rights of minority shareholders and increasing transparency. After the 'Lehman shock' and the world financial crisis, excessive risk taking by management became an additional target of reform initiatives (Kirkpatrick 2009).

At first sight, Japan's recent 'growth oriented' governance reform resembles the above. The emphasis on independent outside directors and on the engagement of institutional investors seems fully in line with governance reform agendas in other countries. However, the concern underling 'seme no gabanansu' is not the prevention of scandals or the strong risk appetite of management. 'The code does not place excessive emphasis on avoiding and limiting risk or the prevention of corporate scandals' (JGC, par. 7). Instead, Principle 4.2 states that the 'board should view the establishment of an environment that supports appropriate risk-taking by the senior management a major aspect of its roles and responsibilities.' These statements raise three questions. Why do lawmakers in Japan think that:

- top managers of Japan's listed companies are too risk averse,
- more risk taking would benefit the economy,
- can be achieved by appointing independent outside directors and by having institutional investors engaging more with their investees.

There is no explicit answer to these questions in the documents explaining the reform initiatives, but because the reforms are part of Japan's revitalization strategy, the first two questions directly relate to the performance puzzle described in the previous subchapter. In particular, the observation that corporations are reluctant to undertake more investment and to expand abroad despite the fact that they hold plenty of cash can be seen as an indication of the kind of risk aversion that the reforms intend to remedy.

The answer to the third question might be constructed along the following reasoning. (1) Boards and institutional investors influence the way top management uses corporate resources. (2a) The main difference between corporate boards in

Japan and elsewhere is their lack of independent outside directors, and (2b) institutional investors engage less with management in Japan than elsewhere. (3) Introducing independent outside directors and encouraging engagement by institutional investors will improve the management of corporate resources. Statement (1) is the least questionable, although (or because) the important aspects of 'to what extent' and 'how' are not addressed. Statements (2a) and (2b) are basically empirical. (2a) is supported by empirical evidence. Japanese boards are dominated by insiders, i.e. by directors with a life-long in-house career (Learmount 2002, pp. 125–129, Dore 2007). (2b) is also supported by research, although even in shareholder friendly corporate governance systems like the UK, institutional investors seem reluctant to actively engage in dialogue with management (Share Action 2015).

The concluding statement (3) is the most intricate, but also the most relevant for the analysis to follow. Empirical research on the relationship between board composition and performance does not provide strong and consistent support for the hypothesis that more independent boards improve performance (Bebchuck and Weisbach 2010, pp. 943–945). This 'non-result' is not surprising, because board composition is not an exogenous variable. Board members are appointed by shareholders at shareholder meetings. Shareholders can be expected to decide the composition of boards in their best interest. Board compositions that systematically harm performance would thus be avoided or corrected. Observed variations in board composition would then not correlate with performance, but would instead reflect company or industry specific conditions.[6] Of course, the same argument can be applied to question regulations that oblige shareholders to appoint independent directors. In fact, the Japanese industry association Keidanren has regularly used such a kind of reasoning in its opposition to legally prescribed numbers for outside directors (Keidanren 2009).

If one suggests that the composition of Japanese boards is not optimal, as the concept of 'seme no gabanansu' does, one needs to point to some structural obstacle that prevents Japanese shareholders from choosing 'better' boards or, in other words, that makes them choose insider dominated boards. The next step would then be to show how such insider boards and/or the underlying factor inducing them have contributed to the underperformance of the economy. In the following, it will be argued that the in-house careers predominant in Japan's large companies represent a structural factor that not only implies insider-dominated boards, but can also be blamed for the weak performance of Japan's economy over the last two decades.

3.2. In-house careers – a central pillar of Japanese corporate governance

As the name suggests, an in-house career means that an employee spends his or her whole career with one company. In-house careers appeared in Japan in the pre-war period (Gordon 1985, pp. 81–107, Nishiguchi 1994, pp. 19–28). In response to the necessity to retain in-house trained employees, companies in the heavy industries such as shipbuilding and steel production offered their core employees wage increases and promotion opportunities to induce them to stay. After the war, unions fought successfully to have their demands for employment stability and for wages based on needs rather than productivity accepted by industry (Gordon 1985, pp. 374–411). The ensuing period of high growth combined with a then very young working population made it easy and even beneficial for companies to commit to lifetime employment and salaries that would increase with the years of service.

In-house careers imply lifetime employment, but the two institutions differ in important aspects. First, most lifetime employees do not make it to the very top of the corporate hierarchy. Second, starting in the mid-1970s, the once favourable growth and demographic conditions steadily worsened, and companies have been steadily reducing their commitment to lifetime employment by increasingly limiting the number of core employees (Waldenberger 2004, pp. 94–96). They nevertheless continue to preserve in-house careers for their core employees.

In-house careers also exist in other economies. The natural choice when it comes to filling higher ranks is to choose in-house candidates from lower ranks. However, whereas in other advanced economies, in-house promotions are only considered as a first option, they represent a quasi rule in Japan. Their predominance can best be seen when looking at the top of the career ladder. Top management positions in Japan, including the board of directors, are almost exclusively reserved to employees with a lifelong career in the company (Miwa 1996, pp. 204–205, Learmount 2002, pp. 125–129, Dore 2007). In other countries, top managers tend to have moved at least once among employers (Waldenberger 2004, pp. 79–80). In the US and Europe, companies tend to fill even the highest corporate rank in one third of all cases with an outside candidate. In Japan, such outside appointments occur only in five per cent of all cases, typically when a company suffers severe distress (Waldenberger 2013, p. 201). Other empirical manifestations of the predominance of in-house careers are:[7]

- a very low turnover rate for skilled and managerial labour, that is even lower than the average turnover rate for all employees,
- a significant loss of lifetime income for most industries and professions when moving to another employer.

It is important to note that in-house careers once having been established as the predominant career pattern are no longer subject to individual choices. If most companies are committed to in-house promotions, it becomes hard to continue one's career successfully with another company or to recruit a talented manager from outside. At least equally important are the implications that in-house careers have for human resource development and decision-making. In-house careers encounter the fundamental problem of matching core employees and tasks. Companies need to ensure that they have tasks for their long-term employees as these move within the organization, and they must have in-house employees capable to perform new upcoming tasks. To solve the problem, training of core employees will be broad so that people and tasks can be more flexibly matched (Aoki 1988, pp. 11–26). With in-house careers being the rule, business decisions become more consensus oriented because it is 'everybody's' company and because disagreement with decisions cannot be simply resolved by leaving the company, instead it will create frustration that stays within the organization. Broad in-house training and consensus-oriented decision-making re-enforce in-house careers. The qualifications gained through in-house training are difficult to 'prove' or testify to other potential employers (Waldenberger 2003, pp. 63–64). Consensus decision-making benefits from good personal relations within the organization that will be lost when moving to another company. Thus, people who move will be less effective consensus arrangers and therefore less qualified for top management positions in the new company.

An employment system where in-house careers are the rule bears three implications for corporate governance. First, the successful completion of one's career becomes conditioned on the survival of one's company. The only way to ensure survival is profitability. Survival is not identical to profit maximization, but in a complex and dynamically changing market environment, it will be hard to distinguish profit maximizing and survival strategies. In any case, a system wide establishment of in-house careers is able to align management and shareholder interests in the pursuit of profits. It is not surprising that shareholders in Japan were never much concerned about monitoring management (Aoki 1988, pp. 142–149). They must have felt assured that managers would do their best to keep the company profitable in order to secure their own future career. Second, when the protection of in-house careers acquires highest priority, corporate strategies will necessarily become long-term oriented and prioritize employment stability over short-term profits (Yoshimori 1995). Third, in-house careers imply boards that are dominated by directors with lifelong in-house careers. In fact, Japanese companies continue to consider board membership as the highest rank of a successful in-house career (Dore 2007). As a result, boards in Japan tended to be very large so that this reward could be offered to a large number of accomplished employees. For a long time the practice created confusion about the function of boards. It is only since the end of the 1990s that monitoring and management functions of boards became more clearly delineated (Dore 2007). Still, the important point is that Japan's insider dominated boards have not been a choice for shareholders, but the natural outcome of an employment system characterized by in-house careers.

3.3. In-house careers and the performance puzzle

How can in-house careers explain Japan's performance puzzle? The question is especially intriguing because in-house careers are closely related to Japan's post-war 'economic miracle'. They became not only established as the dominant career pattern during the high growth period between the early 1950s and the early 1970s, they also supported Japan's industrial and technological catch-up in important ways. The prospects of long-term employment made companies willing to invest in their workforce, while seniority-based wages and promotions created strong incentives for learning among employees (Aoki 1988, Koike 1994). Last, but not least, the long-term affiliation with one company provided an ideal context for organizational learning needed to effectively absorb foreign technology (Cole 1994). After the high-growth period, some industries, especially machinery industries, continued to benefit from organizational learning while others no longer did. As a result, the Japanese economy developed a very strong comparative advantage in machinery, transport equipment and precision instrument industries (Komiya 1999, pp. 93–155). Entering the 1990s, even Japan's export industries lost the dynamic momentum to stimulate overall economic growth. In a low growth environment, the disadvantages of in-house careers became increasingly apparent. They relate to four areas – risk taking, internationalization, diversity and restructuring.

Risk taking. It has already been pointed out that in-house careers create strong incentives for managers to secure the survival of their company, with the positive effect that management and shareholder interests get aligned. However, tying the career risk of core employees to the risk of bankruptcy is likely to make top management more risk averse. This will not become evident as long as there exists a potential to grow along non-disruptive technological trajectories. They allow companies to pursue strategies that combine innovation and growth without putting in-house careers at risk. When such trajectories get depleted, hoarding of cash might be the most natural way to assure survival. This would suggest that the risk aversion 'seme no gabanansu' wants to correct, is less a matter of changing board composition and managerial mind-sets, but much more deeply rooted in the institution of in-house careers.

Internationalization. Companies can exploit their superior know-how on a global scale by selling or licensing their technology, by exporting products and services or by establishing subsidiaries abroad to sell, produce, procure or conduct research and development. The last strategy implies outward foreign direct investment (FDI). It requires the strongest commitment of resources and affords the highest risk. Textbooks on international business suggest a two-stage process, whereby companies first trade and – once their foreign trade volume reaches a certain threshold – start to set up their own operations (Rugman and Collinson 2012, pp. 41–43). FDI does not necessarily substitute for trade, but often enhances it, because own operations provide closer contact to local suppliers and customers abroad. The simultaneous decline of Japan's share in global exports and its share in the stock of outward FDI can be seen as a reflection of the complementary relationship. In other words, explaining Japan's weaker FDI position will also contribute to understanding its weaker export performance.

Successful international operations depend on, among other things, the ability to gain and retain talented personnel in the host country. In-house careers put Japanese companies at a disadvantage in this respect (Iwatani et al 2011, Nagai 2012, Pudelko and Tenzer 2013). They are basically reserved to young talent recruited in Japan and do not grant foreign employees access to top management positions at the home headquarters. Talented and ambitious foreign workers will thus either not join or not stay with Japanese multinationals. The intra-organizational boundaries between headquarters and subsidiaries created by Japan-centred in-house careers draw a strict distinction between employees at the headquarters and employees abroad, which is likely to interfere with the establishment of mutual trust and the free exchange of information necessary for exploiting the synergies from global operations (Beechler et al. 2005). Both the difficulties in gaining and retaining global talent and in integrating global operations can at least partly explain why Japanese companies have been less able to keep pace with the expansion of the global economy over the last two decades.

Diversity. In-house careers exert a strong bias for homogeneity. Homogeneity makes it easier to reach consensus and reduces the risk that people will not get along with each other. Such risk is more relevant and the need for harmony is more pronounced in a context where conflict cannot be resolved by simply exiting the organization. This is already apparent in the way Japanese companies recruit new graduates in Japan (Works Institute 2010). The process, known as 'shûshoku katsudô' (job search) from the students' side, and as 'ikkatsu saiyô' (one-time recruitment) from the employers' side, takes about one year and comprises numerous personal contacts, workshops and recently also short internships, so that each side can get know the other side before they commit to a long-term relationship.

The bias towards homogeneity is further strengthened by the fact that in-house careers per se discriminate against outsiders, such as foreigners who did not enter the system at the headquarters, women who interrupted their career, mid-term hires who changed employer and elderly workers who reached the internal retirement age. As a result, Japanese boards and even lower level decision makers are not in a position to benefit from the virtues of diversity in terms of gender, career background, nationality and age postulated by management research (Hunt et al 2015). The lack of diversity becomes especially severe for companies who operate in an international, dynamically changing environment where management decisions benefit most from incorporating different perspectives and experiences (Upadhyay 2014). And this might be one of the causes for Japan's performance puzzle. As with risk taking, increasing diversity is not a matter of changing managerial mind-sets and boards, but of challenging the predominance of in-house careers and creating a culture that accepts constructive conflict arising from diverse backgrounds as the benefits of diversity cannot be gained by simply setting quotas for different groups (Rhode and Packel 2014).

Restructuring. Productivity is not only a question of how resources are managed at the firm level. It is at least as much the outcome of mechanisms that reallocate resources between companies, ideally moving them from low-performing to better-performing employers. The two basic mechanisms are

- competition among existing companies whereby well-performing companies gain shares at the cost of underperforming companies; in the extreme case, an underperforming company exits the market or is taken over by a better performing competitor;
- competition by new companies, either domestic start-ups or foreign entrants that bring in better techniques, products or business models.

Research on the productivity effects of changes in the firm composition of Japanese industries shows that the growth, entry and exit of firms has not always been productivity increasing as standard competition theory would expect (Fukao 2013). The striking finding corroborates Japan's performance puzzle. It can be at least partly explained by in-house careers for the following reasons. First, in-house careers increase exit barriers. Companies committed to long-term employment will not lay-off their core employees, while the latter will accept wage cuts before leaving the sinking ship. Second, mergers and acquisition are more difficult to successfully implement in Japan as the merged company is faced with the problem of integrating two separate personnel systems that have been formed and functioning on premises that outsiders are not included on equal terms. Third, newly entering firms, be it domestic start-ups or foreign companies setting up a subsidiary in Japan, confront the problem that there is only a limited pool of skilled workers and managers as most of them are stuck in a career with larger incumbent companies.

It is impossible to quantify the performance implications of an employment system characterized by in-house careers operating in a low-growth environment. The arguments made above however suggest that in-house careers with their impact on risk-taking, internationalization, diversity and restructuring must be considered as an important structural factor when explaining Japan's performance puzzle.

4. Implications

The above analysis suggests that the link between corporate governance and economic performance postulated by recent governance reforms is spurious. Both Japanese corporate governance and the underperformance of the economy over the last two decades can be related to a third factor, namely the predominance of in-house careers. It is important to seriously consider this distinguishing characteristic of Japanese business when devising policies at the legislative and corporate level in order to address the performance issue.

To be precise, it is not in-house careers per se, but their predominance that needs to be corrected in order to revitalize the Japanese economy. It means giving companies the option to hire and promote outsiders to top managerial ranks, and allowing employees to change employers without damaging their career prospects. The challenge is to balance in-house promotions with a functioning labour market for managerial labour as in other economies. The decoupling of management careers from company risk will make boards and top management less risk averse. The opening up of in-house careers to outsiders will make it easier for Japanese companies to take advantage of the competences of women, foreigners and aged workers. The mobility of skilled and managerial labour will also support the reallocation of resources within and across industries through exit, mergers and acquisitions and the entry of new start-ups and foreign companies.

The governance reforms address the right problem, but the measures applied, like the demand for a minimum number of independent board members and a constructive dialogue between institutional investors and management, can only scratch the surface. Seen in isolation they are not likely to be effective, even if implemented. The composition and functioning of Japanese boards is conditioned by the predominance of in-house careers. Insider-dominated boards are therefore not the final cause of Japan's performance puzzle.

Constituting a structural factor, the predominance of in-house careers cannot be changed by law or by single actions of specific companies. Change can come through established companies, such as Nomura Holdings or Takeda Pharmaceuticals, which having made big acquisitions abroad find themselves confronted with the challenges of retaining and effectively integrating a large group of foreign employees.[8] In addition, younger, still founder-managed companies with a strong international orientation, such as Softbank or more recently Rakuten, are taking a more open and flexible approach to the management and development of human resources.

The governance reforms can play an important role in promoting such developments. The inclusion of independent outside directors forms a natural complement to the opening up of in-house careers. A similar positive stimulus will result from encouraging institutional investors to engage with management in a dialogue about human resource management strategies.

Disclosure statement

No potential conflict of interest was reported by the author.

Notes

1. The Government of Japan established a special website for 'Abenomics' to explain about the content with regard to planned policy measures and about their implementation, see http://www.japan.go.jp/abenomics/index.html (accessed 30 October 2015). Updates of the 'Japan Revitalization Strategy' are separately documented on the website of the Cabinet Office http://japan.kantei.go.jp/97_abe/Documents/2015/index.html.
2. The official documents do not further elaborate the assumption. Possible interpretations and evidence underlying the assumptions are provided in Section 3.1.
3. *The Economist* (6 June 2015), Business in Japan. Meet Shinzo Abe, the shareholder activist. At last Japan has introduced corporate governance reforms that will make a difference, http://www.economist.com/node/21653610/print (accessed 31 October 2015). *The Wall Street Journal* (2 June 2015), Japan's New Code of Conduct. Defining principles and practices for the way companies do business, by Nick Benes.
4. For an exception see Miyajima (2015).
5. Between the end of 1997 and the end of 2013 Japan's private non-financial corporate sector improved its net financial assets position by 110 trillion yen (own calculations based on Bank of Japan, Flow of Funds Statistics, http://www.boj.or.jp/en/statistics/sj/index.htm/ (accessed 30 October 2015).
6. Hermalin and Weisbach (2006) in their evaluation of governance reforms argue similarly that governance structures are endogenously determined.
7. See Waldenberger (2013 p. 201)
8. *Japan Times* (26 March 2011), Firms urged to develop leaders in global business environment, by Takashi Kitazume; *Japan Times* (11 August 2014), Takeda Pharmaceuticals to stay Japan-based while growing on global basis, new French leader vows, by Atsushi Kodera.

References

Aguilera, R. V. and Jackson, G., 2003. The cross-national diversity of corporate governance. *Dimensions and Determinants, in: The academy of management review*, 28 (3), 447–465.

Aoki, M., 1988. *Information, Incentives and Bargaining in the Japanese Economy*. New York: Cambridge University Press.

Aoki, M., 1994. The Japanese firm as a system of attributes: a survey and research agenda. *in:* M. Aoki and R. Dore, eds. *The Japanese firm. sources of competitive strength*. Oxford: Oxford University Press, 11–40.

Aoki, M., Jackson, G., and Miyajima, H. eds., 2007. *Corporate governance in Japan. Institutional change and organizational diversity*. Oxford: Oxford University Press.

Aoyagi, C. and Ganelli, G., 2013. Path to Higher Growth. Does Revamping Japan's Dual Labor Market Matter? IMF Working Paper WP/13/202, International Monetary Fund.

Bebchuk, L. A. and Weisbach, M. S., 2010. The State of Corporate Governance Research. Review of Financial Studies 23 (3), 939–961.

Beechler, S., et al., 2005. Does it really matter if Japanese MNCs think globally? *In:* T. Roehl and A. Bird, eds. *Japanese firms in transition: responding to the globalization challenge*. Bingley: Emerald Group Publishing, 261–288.

Cabinet Office 2015. Outline of Revitalization Strategy – Revised in 2015. Available from: http://japan.kantei.go.jp/index.html, [Accessed 30 October 2015].

Cole, R. E., 1994. Different Quality Paradigms and their implication for organizational learning. *In:* M. Aoki and R. Dore, eds. *The Japanese firm. The sources of competitive strength.* New York: Oxford University Press, 66–83.

Committee on the Financial Aspects of Corporate Governance 1992. *Report of the committee on the financial aspects of corporate governance (Cadbury report)*. London: Gee, Available from: http://www.ecgi.org/codes/documents/cadbury.pdf, [Accessed 1 November 2015].

Council of Experts Concerning the Japanese Version of the Stewardship Code 2014. Principles for Responsible Institutional Investors – Japan's Stewardship Code – To promote sustainable growth of companies through investment and dialogue, 26 February 2014, Available from: http://www.fsa.go.jp/en/refer/councils/stewardship/20140407/01.pdf, [Accessed 30 October 2015].

Council of Experts Concerning the Corporate Governance Code 2015. Japan's Corporate Governance Code [Final Proposal]. Seeking Sustainable Corporate Growth and Increased Corporate Value over the Mid- to Long-Term, 5 March 2015, Available from: http://www.fsa.go.jp/en/refer/councils/corporategovernance/20150306-1/01.pdf.

Dernis, H. and Khan, M., 2004. Triadic Patent Families Methodology. OECD Science, Technology and Industry Working Papers 2004/2. Paris: OECD.

Dore, R., 1988. Flexible rigidities. *Industrial Policy and Structural Adjustment in the Japanese Economy.* London: The Athlone Press.

Dore, R., 2000. *Stock market capitalism – welfare capitalism. Japan and Germany versus the Anglo-Saxons.* Oxford: Oxford University Press.

Dore, R., 2007. Insider management and board reform: For whose benefit? *In*: M. Aoki, G. Jackson, and H. Miyajima, eds. *Corporate governance in Japan. Institutional change and organizational diversity.* Oxford: Oxford University Press, 370–397.

Ethier, W. J., 1982. National and international returns to scale in the modern theory of international trade. *The American Economic Review*, 72 (3), 389–405.

Fukao, K., 2013. Explaining Japan's unproductive two decades. *Asian Economic Policy Review* 8, 193–213.

Gilson, R. J. and Roe, M. J., 1999. Lifetime employment. Labor peace and the evolution of Japanese corporate goverance. *Columbia Law Review* 99 (2), 508–540.

Gordon, A., 1985. *The evolution of labor relations in Japan. Heavy Industry, 1853–1955.* Cambridge, Mass.: Harvard University Press.

Goto, G., 2013. The outline for the companies act reform in Japan and its implications. *Journal of Japanese Law*, 35, 13–38.

Government of Japan 2015. Abenomics is progressing. *Towards the Reinvigoration of the Japanese Economy.* October 2015, Available from: http://www.japan.go.jp/_userdata/abenomics/abenomics_151007.pdf, [Accessed 30 October 2015].

Head, K., Ries, J., 2004. Exporting and FDI as alternative strategies. *Oxford Review of Economic Policy*, 20 (3), 409–423.

Hermalin, B. E. and Weisbach, M. S., 2006. A framework for assessing corporate governance reform. NBER Working Paper No. 12050, Available from: http://www.nber.org/papers/w12050, [Accessed 1 November 2015].

Hunt, V., Layton, D., and Prince, S., 2015. *Diversity matters.* McKinsey & Company, Available from: http://www.mckinsey.com/business-functions/organization/our-insights/why-diversity-matters, [Accessed 3 February 2017].

Imai, K. and Komiya R., 1994. *Business enterprise in Japan. Views of leading Japanese economists.* Cambridge, Mass.: MIT Press.

Iwatani, N., Orr, G., and Salsberg, B., 2011 Japan's globalization imperative. *McKinsey quarterly*, June 2011, 1–11.

Jackson, G. and Miyajima, H., 2007. Introduction. The diversity and change of corporate governance in Japan. *In*: M. Aoki, G. Jackson, and H. Miyajima, eds. *Corporate Governance in Japan. Institutional Change and Organizational Diversity*. Oxford: Oxford University Press, 1–49.

Jones, R. S. and Urasawa, S., 2011. Labour Market Reforms in Japan to Improve Growth and Equity. OECD Economic Department Working Papers NO 889. Paris: OECD.

Keidanren 2009. *Towards better corporate governance. Interim discussion paper on key issues*. Tokyo: Nippon Keidanren, Available from: https://www.keidanren.or.jp/english/policy/2009/038.pdf, [Accessed 1 November 2015].

Kirkpatrick, G., 2009. The corporate governance lessons from the financial crisis. *Financial Market Trends* 96 (1), Available from: http://www.oecd.org/finance/financial-markets/42229620.pdf, [Accessed 1 November 2015].

Koike, K., 1994. Learning and incentive systems in Japanese industry. *In:* M. Aoki and R. Dore, eds. *The Japanese Firm. The sources of competitive strength*. New York: Oxford University Press, 41–65.

Komiya, R., 1999. *Nihon no sangyô, bôeki no keizai bunseki [Economic analysis of Japanese industry and trade]*. Tokyo: Tôyô Keizai Shinpôsha.

Koo, R., 2003. *Balance sheet recession. Japan's struggle with uncharted economics and its global implications*. Singapore: John Wiley and Sons.

Learmount, S., 2002. *Corporate governance. What can be learned from Japan?* Oxford: Oxford University Press.

Milhaupt, C. J. and West, M. D., 2004. *Economic organization and corporate governance in Japan: The impact of formal and informal rules*. Oxford: Oxford University Press.

Miwa, Y., 1996. *Firms and industrial organization in Japan*. Basingstoke: Macmillan.

Miyajima, H., 2015. Kigyô tôchi seido kaikaku no shiten. Haiburiddona kôzô no fainchûningu to retsui no kinkô kara no dasshutsu ni mukete [A view on corporate governance system reform. Towards finetuning of hybrid structures and escape from an inferior equilibrium], RIETI Policy Discussion Paper Series 15-P-011. Tokyo: RIETI.

Nagai, H., 2012. Nihon kigyô ni okeru gurôbaru jinzai ikusei shisutemu no kôchiku ni mukete [Towards the establishment of a global human resource development system in Japanese companies]. *Nihon Rôdô Kenkyû Zasshi* 623, 17–28.

Nakamura, N., 2015. Amendment to the company law and corporate governance reform of listed companies. Waseda University Institute of Comparative Law, Available from: http://www.waseda.jp/hiken/en/jalaw_inf/topics2013/topic/002nakamura.html, [Accessed 4 May 2015].

Nicoletti, G., et al., 2003. The influence of policies on trade and foreign direct investment. *OECD Economic Studies*, 36, 7–83.

Nishiguchi, T., 1994. *Strategic industrial sourcing. The Japanese advantage*. New York: Oxford University Press.

Odagiri, H., 1994. *Growth through competition, competition through growth. Strategic management and the economy in Japan*. Oxford: Clarendon Press.

OECD 2004. *OECD principles of corporate governance*. Paris: OECD.

OECD 2012. *Policies for a revitalisation of Japan*. Paris: OECD.

OECD 2013. *OECD skills outlook 2013*. Paris: OECD.

OECD 2014. *Education at a glance 2014. OECD indicators*. Paris: OECD.

OECD 2015a. *OECD economic surveys Japan*. Paris: OECD.

OECD 2015b. *OECD compendium of productivity indicators 2015*. Paris: OECD.

Posen, A. S., 1998. *Restoring Japan's economic growth*. Washington: Institute for International Economics.

Pudelko, M. and Tenzer, H., 2013. Subsidiary control in Japanese, German and US multinational corporations: Direct control from headquarters versus indirect control through expatriation. *Asian, Business and Management*, 12, 409–431.

Rhode, D. L. and Packel, A. K., 2014. Diversity on corporate boards: how much difference does difference make? *Delaware Journal of Corporate Law*, 39, 377–425.

Rugman, A. M. and Collinson, S., 2012. *International Business*. 6th ed. London: Pearson.

Share Action 2015. *The 2015 share action survey. Responsible investment performance of UK asset managers*. London: ShareAction.

Shishido, Z., 2001. Reform in Japanese corporate law and corporate governance. Current changes in historical perspective. *The American Journal of Comparative Law*, 49, 653–678.

Shishido, Z., 2004. Changes in Japanese corporate law and governance. Revisiting the convergence debate. University of Berkeley, eScholarship Repository, Available from: http://escholarship.org/uc/item/9376480h, [Accessed 5 May 2014].

Shishido, Z., 2007. The turnaround of 1997: Changes in Japanese corporate law and governance. *In*: M. Aoki, G. Jackson, and H. Miyajima, eds. *Corporate governance in Japan. Institutional change and organizational diversity*. Oxford: Oxford University Press, 310–329.

Upadhyay, A., 2014. Social concentration on boards, Corporate information environment and cost of capital. *Journal of Business Finance and Accounting*, 41, 974–1001.

Waldenberger, F., 2003. *The link between finance and employment, in: regulation, competition and the market economy*. Göttingen: Vandehoeck &Ruprecht, 61–75.

Waldenberger, F., 2004. Changes in the Japanese employment system – facts and speculations, *In:* G. Foljanty-Jost, ed. *Japan in the 1990s. Crisis as an impetus for change*. Münster: LIT Verlag, 77–101.

Waldenberger, F., 2013. "Company heroes " versus" Superstars" – Executive pay in Japan in comparative perspective. *Contemporary Japan*, 25, 189–213.

Waldenberger, F., 2014. Japan's new monetary policy: Some critical questions, *In*: F. Roevekamp and H. G. Hilpert, eds. *Currency cooperation in East Asia*. Heidelberg: Springer, 43–55.

Whittaker, D.H. and Simon, D., eds. 2009. *Corporate governance and managerial reform in Japan*. Oxford: Oxford University Press.

Works Institute 2010. *'Shinsotsu saiyou' no chôryû to kadai [Trend and problems of hiring new graduates]*. Tokyo: Recruit.

Yashiro, N., 2011. Myths about Japanese employment practices. An increasing insider-outsider conflict of interest. *Contemporary Japan*, 23, 133–155.

Yoshimori, M., 1995. Whose company is it? The Concept of the Corporation in Japan and the West. *Long Range Planning*, 28, 33–44.

Young, Allen, 1928. Increasing returns and economic progress. *The Economic Journal*, 38, 527–542.

Appendix

Table A1 List of OECD countries included in the resource conditions and performance comparison (in alphabetic order).

1	Australia
2	Austria
3	Belgium
4	Canada
5	Denmark
6	Finland
7	France
8	Germany
9	Ireland
10	Italy
11	Japan
12	Korea
13	Netherlands
14	New Zealand
15	Spain
16	Sweden
17	Switzerland
18	United Kingdom
19	United States

The Japanese consumer finance market and its institutional changes since the 1980s

ADRIENNE SALA

Abstract: We assert, in this article, that the joint transformation of public perception about households' over-indebtedness and financial deregulation had important implications on the government decision to reform overall consumer credit between 2005 and 2010. On the one hand, the development of collective actions by groups of lawyers to defend borrowers from moneylenders' abusive practices represents a source of change in the public opinion about over-indebted individuals in the context of long economic stagnation. A systematic press article analysis from 1977 to 2006 shows that the rising number of these collective actions since the early 1990s may have gradually increased the political salience of social issues related to the unsecure loan market. On the other hand, financial deregulation has been a source of change by allowing banks to enter the consumer finance market since the early 2000s. Banks entry into this market transformed the logic of complementarity among traditional consumer credit actors (Shinpan, credit card companies and *sarakin*) in a general context of legal consumers' protection reinforcement. Thus, evolution of Japanese consumer finance's regulation is particularly relevant to illustrate the forces of institutional change and its consequences.

1. Introduction

Since the 1980s, excessive household debt has gradually become a serious social and political challenge in many advanced countries. The number of personal bankruptcies increased in the United States as well as in countries with a more 'conservative' private debt policy, such as France and Germany (Sullivan et al. 2000, Niemi and Whitford 2009, Garon 2011, Hyman 2011, Logemann 2012, Trumbull 2014).[1] In addition, many governments responded by revising their insolvency procedure in order to ease the process and at the same time reduce the social stigma attached to personal bankruptcy (Posner 1995, White 2007a). In comparison, in Japan, scholarly interest both in consumer credit and households' over-borrowing has been, until recently, relatively low. The three most common explanations are that until the end of the 1990s, the Japanese economy was characterized by a high rate of saving (Horioka 1990); Japanese households hate getting into debt, partly due to the social trauma attached to personal bankruptcy (West 2005); and Japanese banks were late in entering the consumer credit market (Horioka 1990, Hoshi & Kashyap 2001).[2] In fact, during the lost decade (1992–2004), on aggregate, debt driven consumption did not increase among Japanese households and the ratio of debt to income remained stagnant since the early 1990s,[3] as Japanese households used their savings to maintain a certain level of consumption (Kobayashi & Ono 2010). However, according to the Nichibenren annual reports, since the mid-1990s households' indebtedness increased among lower income bracket as a result of over-borrowing on the non-bank unsecure loan market.[4] In 2006, in order to solve the over-borrowing and excess of lending problem (*tajûsaimu*), the Koizumi's government implemented the revision of the Moneylenders Business Law (*kashikingyô hô*, 1983) to reinforce the regulation of the overall consumer finance market.

The 2007–2008 subprime loan financial crisis contributed to a renewed interest regarding consumer credit and, more broadly, the history of American capitalism (e.g. Graeber 2014, Hyman 2011), whereas after the burst of the housing and financial bubble (1989–1991) the rise of Japanese consumer finance market and the increase of personal bankruptcies did not trigger the same level of interest among social sciences scholars. Nevertheless, the new Moneylenders' business law (*kaisei kashikingyô hô*) voted on in 2006 and fully implemented in 2010 has been analyzed, especially among jurists. They emphasize the role of the judiciary power in the government's decision to reform the consumer finance market and they also stress the lower bargaining power of Consumer Finance Companies (the so-called *sarakin*), which I shall refer to as CFCs (Kozuka & Nottage 2007, 2009, Pardieck 2008, Ramseyer 2013). These studies contribute to the consumer credit literature by shedding light on the Japanese case in comparative analysis. But the process of institutional change that occurred in this market, historically dominated by moneylenders,[5] is yet to be analyzed. Indeed, moneylenders were organized into pressure groups enjoying a high political influence, in contrast with the lack of borrowers' political representation (*weak interest*). Moneylenders including CFCs developed informal practices of lending due to an ambiguity of the consumer finance regulation. In addition, the lack of a legal concept of 'over-indebtedness', the low level of consumers' legal protection in the financial sector and the unfriendly insolvency procedure until the end of the 1990s, allowed several moneylenders to conduct abusive lending practices.

In this article, we analyze the institutional transformations of the Japanese consumer finance market by focusing on the evolution of the moneylenders business' regulation since the late 1970s to the late 2000s. By emphasizing the gap between formal rules and informal practices, we look at the rise of several social issues, especially households' over-indebtedness, leading to personal bankruptcy. We analyze more precisely the collective actions organized by groups of lawyers to help indebted persons by providing financial and legal counseling services and how their actions changed the public's perception about over-indebted individuals.

The article is structured as follows. In Section 2, we discuss the literature on consumer credit and introduce briefly the concept of political salience. In Section 3, the chronological and historical perspective allows us to analyze in parallel the rise of the consumer finance market as well as social issues related to over-indebtedness. Section 4 analyzes the evolution of the public debate about the *sarakin mondai*, with a particular focus on collective actions organized by borrowers' advocates and the press coverage. A final section provides a conclusion.

2. Literature on consumer credit and political salience

This section engages with the literature on consumer credit and personal bankruptcy by focusing on the institutional changes that affected the historical complementarity between bank and non-bank sectors in Japan. We also propose to connect the literature on collective actions and social mobilization to analyze the rising influence of the lawyers who represented the borrowers' interest in the legislative and judiciary arenas.

2.1. *The Japanese consumer credit*

Informal small loans in rural popular finance (*shômin kinyû*) have been widely analyzed in the Japanese economic and financial history literature. Historically, moneylenders assumed an important role as an alternative form of informal credit to peasants, individual entrepreneurs and family businesses (Shibuya 1972, 2001). Pawnshops also developed in urban areas at the beginning of the twentieth century, taking opportunities from the rise of the consumer society and lack of regulation (Shibuya 1972, Sala 2015). In the postwar period, many *shichiya* changed their core business to enter the new market of unsecured personal loans (*sarakin*); however, research about this market and its development faded (Gelpi and Labruyère 1994). In comparison, installment sales credit was analyzed much more, especially by historians. Gordon (2006) shows how consumer credit companies developed in the prewar period in collaboration with department stores to propose installment sales credit to the emerging middle-class consumers. Since the 1950s, consumer credit companies developed new credit facilities to consumers with bank accounts[6] (Partner 2000, Gordon 2012). The apparent paradox between Japanese households' high saving rate and the rise of consumerism is partly due to this easy-access to consumer credit during the high economic and income growth period (Partner 2000). Simon Partner shed light on the gap between lower and higher income households' access to mass consumer society as lower income households had very few savings and bought consumer durables on credit, whereas higher income households could be both savers and consumers. These studies show that the economic and social history of the Japanese consumption society is closely related to consumer credit's development in the prewar period (Francks & Hunter 2011, Gordon 2012). In many ways, consumer credit sustained the rise of mass consumption, as observed in other industrialized countries (Calder 1999, Glickman 1999), but the Japanese consumer credit market also shows several institutional characteristics.

2.2. *Institutional characteristics of Japanese consumer credit*

We observe the historically low participation of banks, except during the bubble period of the late 1980s, and a highly segmented overall market which is dependent on the type of credit provided (credit card, installment sales, unsecure loan, mortgage loan). This segmentation has reduced the consumer credit market's efficiency by creating niche markets under different regulation and public authority supervision. Adding to these specific aspects of regulatory and economic landscape, the lack of a centralized credit bureau has contributed to increasing the risk of over-borrowing as well as an excess of lending from small loan lenders who charged legally high interest rates. Although, in comparison with other industrialized countries, Japanese households' ratio of debt to income was low until the end of the 1970s, it significantly increased during the 1980s and then stabilized during the 1990s (Horioka 2012). Nevertheless, we observe a paradox between the aggregate level of secure household debt and the micro-level data showing a rapid increase in the number of bankruptcies in the late 1990s following the reform of the insolvency law (1996–2004). A study of personal bankruptcies factors reveals that the majority of cases are related to over-borrowing on the unsecure loan market (*sarakin*) (Higuchi & Banno 2004). Since the 1980s, groups of lawyers within the Nichibenren (Japan Federation of Bar Associations) have carried out several lobbying campaigns demanding more stringent small loan regulation to protect borrowers from an excess of lending at high interest rates on the unsecured loan market.

2.3. *Collective actions and political salience of Japanese households' over-indebtedness*

Japan is characterized by a State and Industry coalition that reduces civil society's influence over policymakers (Stigler 1971, Trumbull 2014). This approach is nuanced by other studies that are specific to the Japanese case of consumer protection. For example, Maclachlan (2002) argues that, in the rare cases where the interests of politics, bureaucrats and industry are in conflict, consumer groups can find a way to voice their grievances in the public arena and gain political support. However, when there is a strong cohesion of interests between those three groups (politics, bureaucrats and industry), the government pays little heed to consumer groups, even when the public supports them. Calder (1988) highlights a very similar process in favor of consumers during a period of economic crisis in contrast to the general tendency of the Japanese government to privilege producers over consumers. Nevertheless, these studies did not mention how to measure the evolution of the public opinion's interest in the consumers' cause. For example, the concept of political salience gives insights into the variation of the public interest by identifying the importance of a subject for the average voters in comparison with other political issues (Kollman 1998). In a context of high salience of a particular issue, political parties will begin to pay attention to that issue, as will public opinion (Baron 1994). In this context, interest groups will also start launching campaigns to mobilize public interest (Kollman 1998). Based on a large volume of literature concerning interest groups and collective actions, Culpepper shows that in a context of low political salience, concentrated interests have more influence over politics than diffuse interests (Olson 1965, Wilson 1973, Culpepper 2010). The next question, then, is how does a matter of low salience become a matter of high salience? Wilson (1980) argues that public interest can be mobilized more effectively when scandals are covered by the media, especially in periods of economic crisis. The level of media coverage of an issue provides politicians with an indicator to understand which information the public cares about (Patterson 1993). This dynamic approach is helpful to understand how, during the 1990s, collective actions organized by lawyers and covered by the media, gradually influenced the political salience of social issues related to CFCs and small lenders' informal and abusive practices, leading to several scandals.

3. The rise of the Japanese consumer finance market

In the postwar period, banks focused on secured business loans and had little interest in consumer credit. The 1950s saw the emergence of moneylenders, known as *danchi kinyu* (condominium finance), who followed in the legacy of the traditional *shômin kinyû* (popular finance) (Shibuya 2001). Moneylenders could take advantage of a gray zone, created by the legal gap between the interest rate ceiling of 20 per cent, set by the Interest Rate Restriction Act (IRRA, No 100, 1954) under the civil code and the 109.5 per cent ceiling for the interest rate set by the Investment, Deposit and Interest Rates Act (IA No 195, 1954) under the penal code. Both of these laws governed the consumer finance industry. In the 1960s, the number of urban small lenders increased rapidly in the context of consumer and wage-based society's boom. Consumer finance companies provided small and unsecured loans to wage earners. These companies were called *sarakin*, a popular abbreviation of 'salaryman' + 'loan' (*kinyû*). They provided loans that required only an identification card and a self-declaration of income. The market was virtually unregulated, and continued to grow during the 1970s and the 1980s, dominated by four major consumer finance companies, Promise, Acom, Takefuji and Aiful, but also including a large number of small lenders in charge of proving loans to individual entrepreneurs, family business, and retailers (TAPALS 2006).

3.1. Social issues and legislation's ambiguity

During the 1970s, numerous scandals involving high interest lending practices and harsh collection tactics forced the Ministry of Finance (MoF) to adopt regulatory measures in order to address the problem known as *sarakin mondai*, associated with over-borrowing, usury and illicit practices, which in the worst cases led to debt-related suicides.[7] After almost six years of debate, the Money Lending Business Law (MLBL) was passed in 1983 as proposed by the Liberal Democrat Party (LDP). The law set an objective to reduce over time and at 'a future date' the maximum interest rate at 40.0004 per cent. The law also enacted the 'voluntary payment provisions',[8] which remained in force until the Supreme Court definitively ruled against the application of this provision in 2004 (Pardieck 2008) (see Figure 1).

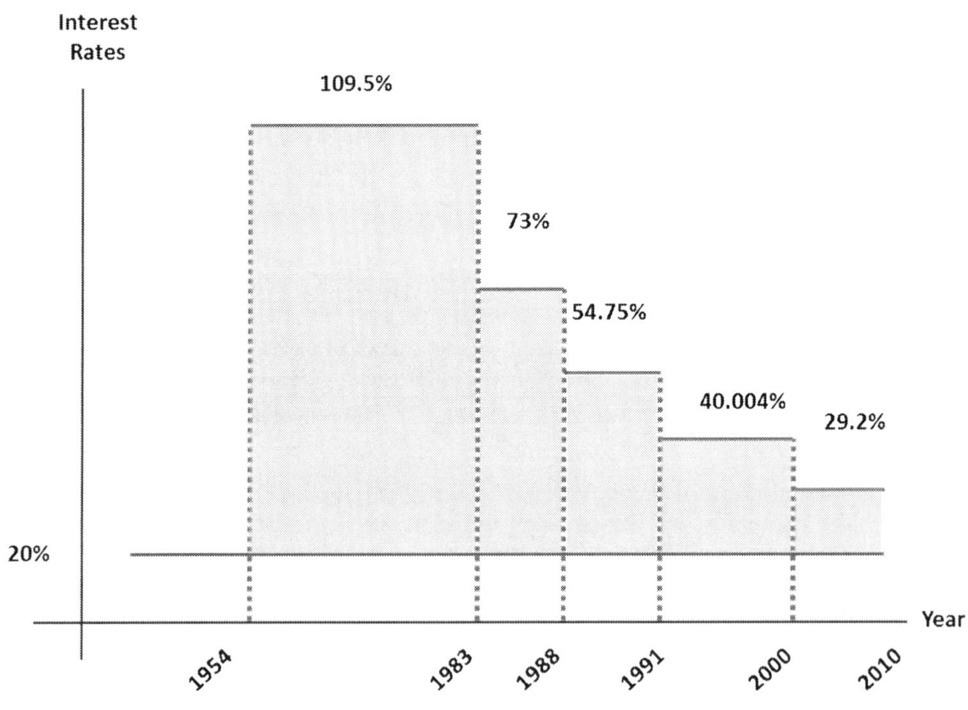

Figure 1 The grey zone of lending from 1954 to 2010
Source: FSA

Opposition parties and several lawyers argued that the law was likely to enlarge the usury pot and was tilted towards protecting the interests of moneylenders.[9] Rules were established in favor of moneylenders' interests, resulting in self-regulatory measures and upholding of the Supreme Court's decisions (1964 and 1968) in favor of borrowers' protection. An accurate study of the Upper house finance committee preceding the vote on the law proposed by the deputy Ohara (DPL) shows that, despite their presence in the legislative arena, borrowers' defense groups (consumers associations and lawyers) could not voice their arguments in favor of more protective legislation for borrowers and a lower interest rate cap ceiling by abolishing the gray zone. The final law was unpopular with the scholars and lawyers involved, partly because of the provision in Article 43 stating that, where the borrower 'voluntary paid interest' in excess of the maximum interest rates and the borrower received the necessary documentation, that payment would be 'deemed a valid payment of interest on the debt'.[10] Article 43 was designed to allow lenders to continue charging higher interest rates during an unspecified period of time. The political collusion between the conservatives (DPL) and the CFCs (*sarakin*) was highly criticized in the newspapers.[11]

The historical informal complementarity between bank and non-bank sectors, which consisted of addressing the demand for credit from high-risk borrowers (SMEs, VSEs, entrepreneurs and family business) to whom banks could not lend, was re-used in the early 1980s to let CFCs make profits by lending large amounts of personal loans at high interest rates to a wider range of consumers. Since the late 1970s and despite the historical complementarity with non-bank lenders, banks have attempted to expand the consumer credit market and shape consumer demand. They became strong advocates of credit access policies. The MoF encouraged banks to practice consumer lending, and revised the banking law in 1984. This coalition was also intended to help shape the consumer finance market by pushing illicit small loan lenders out of the market.[12] By the mid-1980s, consumer credit became more universal and competitive, resulting in a reduced number of peripheral players. For a short period of time, banks became key players in consumer finance and increased their market share on the personal loan sector, whereas CFCs experienced a significant decrease of their business (see Figure 2). The debt (including consumer credit and housing loans) to disposable income ratio increased steadily up to the 1990s (e.g. 77 per cent in 1980, 88.8 per cent in 1985 and 131.5 per cent in 1990).[13] Different factors account for this: growth of personal income, demand for consumer durables, availability of technology providing a better management of credit transactions, as well as financial institutions looking for underdeveloped markets for their accumulated funds (Arthur & Alexander 1989).

At the end of the 1980s, the overall consumer finance market increased significantly as did credit card debt and subprime loans.[14] After the bubble burst, over-indebtedness and personal bankruptcy increased rapidly in a deflationary and economic downturn period.[15] Banks rationed consumer credit, thus providing

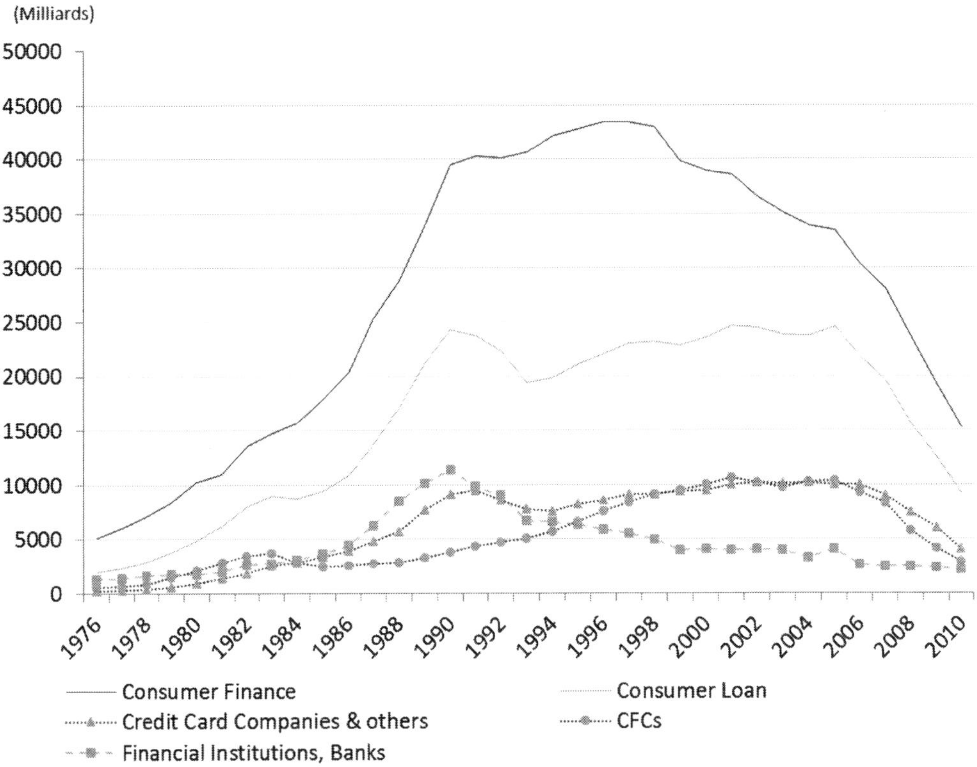

Figure 2 Evolution of the consumer finance market.
Source: Annual reports of the Japan Consumer Credit Association

new market opportunities for consumer finance companies (CFCs) to develop their own markets. Unsecured loans increased again during the so-called lost decade (1992–2004). During this period, CFCs and commercial banks developed strong financial ties and re-enacted the traditional institutional complementarity. The burst of the bubble in a virtually unregulated market led to unintended consequences in favor of Consumer Finance Companies.

3.2. *Rise of consumer finance companies during the lost decade*

After the bubble burst, the relationship between banks and CFCs changed as banks' market shares dramatically decreased in the consumer finance market and CFCs' market shares significantly increased[16] (see Figure 3).

In 1991, in response to several financial scandals, which occurred during the bubble period, the government revised the Investment Act by lowering the ceiling to 40.0004 per cent. As compensation to moneylenders, the MoF authorized CFCs to raise funds directly on the financial market by issuing commercial paper (CP) and

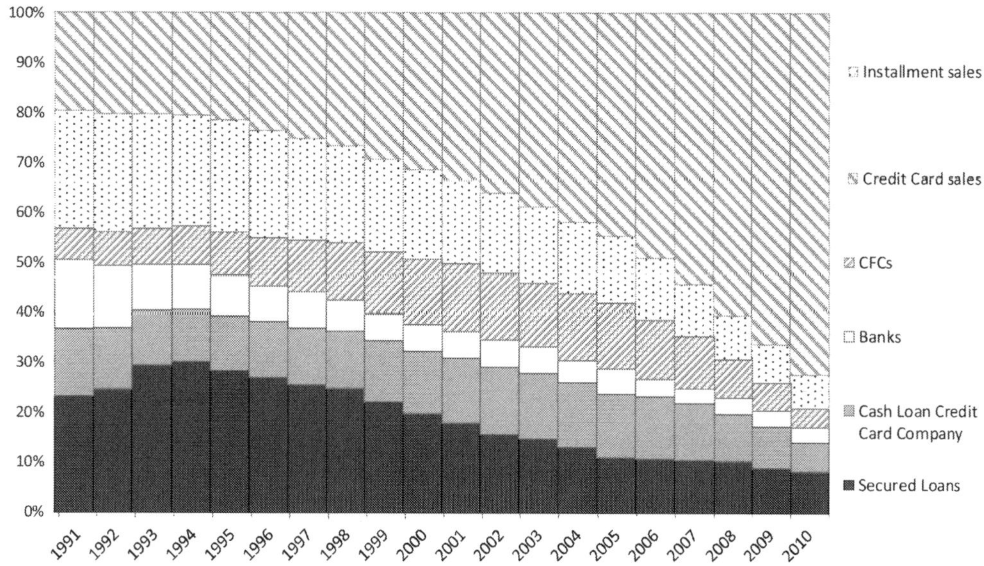

Figure 3 Evolution of the Japanese consumer credit's market shares
Source: Annual reports of the Japan Consumer Credit Association

bonds. Then, in 1999, the revision of the Non-Bank Bond Law allowed the CFCs with capital in excess of 1 billion yen to issue corporate bonds.[17] They were registered as Certified Finance Corporations. During the mid-1990s the major CFCs were also listed on the Tokyo Stock Exchange and by the end of the 1990s, they were accepted into the *Keidenren*.[18] According to Forbes' ranking of the wealthiest people in 2004, there were the four top CFC's directors, ranking second, fifth, sixth and tenth.[19] By the 1990s, banks and CFCs had built strong financial ties, and banks became the CFCs' principal fund suppliers, lending to them at low interest rates (1.70 per cent and 2.50 per cent), and joining them as shareholders.[20] The rise of the CFCs can be attributed to their business model, characterized by a strategy of aggressive credit distribution based on high volume of high-risk borrowers.

At the beginning of the 1990s, advances in telecommunications transformed the economic logic of the sector. CFCs developed an Automatic Teller Machine distribution system to provide credit contracts. This new system increased the number of new clients, lowered the cost of credit, and enhanced easy-access credit. From 1998, the CFCs also improved their distribution network by using convenience store payment terminals and cash withdrawal systems.[21] By the late 1990s, the CFCs had diversified their products strategy by increasing home equity loans, SME loans and equity funds, as well as credit cards.[22] Promise formed an alliance with the Sanwa Bank (then UFJ) to launch Mobito, a consumer credit company targeting middle-risk consumers and in 2000, the Tokyo Mitsubishi Bank developed its credit card, Cash One, in association with Acom. During the same period, the government lifted the ban on advertising and the major CFCs developed more aggressive marketing and advertising campaigns in newspapers and on television.[23]

3.3. Social issues and scandals in a period of economic downturn

Since the 1990s the consumer finance market has been an oligopolistic market with more than 70 per cent of outstanding loans held by a few major CFCs, even though more than 90 per cent of the total number of lenders are small lenders and more than half of them lend money to SMEs.[24] Although the legislation is the same for all moneylenders, this highlights the strong heterogeneity of the market in terms of size and type of borrowers (consumers, SMEs). The role of the Money Lending Business Law was to set rules and regulations to establish control over the lenders. However, the self-regulatory provisions and the lack of government financial control led, again, to a virtually unregulated market. The Japanese government did not enforce any regulation to protect consumers who borrowed money. For example, borrowers' protection in the following three areas of credit market regulation was deficient: there was a lack of transparency in consumer credit contracts, a lack of provision to limit excessive or extortionate lending, and insolvency proceedings were overly long and costly. Although most of the advanced industrialized countries dramatically revised their personal insolvency law, beginning in the mid-1980s, it was the case that the Japan Personal Insolvency Law was only revised in 1996 and fully implemented in 2004. The purpose of the revision was to facilitate the process of filing for personal bankruptcy and to reduce the social stigma associated with it.[25] In addition, there was no regulation of national credit rating agencies: there were four main credit bureaus and, in 2005, only 2079 out of 14,000 registered moneylenders were members of a credit bureau federation.[26] This meant that a large number of lenders were not using established credit bureaus and their borrowers were not included in official statistics.[27]

In the context of economic stagnation and banking crisis, the 1990s bore witness to several scandals. As of 1998, when banks started to ration credit, unsecured loans to SMEs increased, as well as illicit and harsh practices leading to the so-called *shôkôron mondai*. The government took action by lowering the ceiling on interest rates to 29.2 per cent in 2000, but it did not abolish the gray zone, neither did it revise the credit policy to provide better access to credit as well as legal protection for borrowers. In response to the lower ceiling on interest rates, large CFCs sought more volume in order to maintain their profits (Utsunomiya 2007). Low regulation and lack of a centralized data system (credit bureau) led to an excess of lending: in the worst cases, borrowers were receiving credit from more than ten lenders (Suda 2006).[28] Debtors, who found themselves in trouble, having borrowed money from CFCs, often went to smaller lenders to borrow money to reimburse the previous loan, and in the worst cases they borrowed from predatory lenders, known as *yamikin*.[29]

4. Collective actions and political salience

An increase of over-indebtedness may threaten the expansion of the virtually unregulated consumer finance market as a result of an increasing general concern over the problem. In addition, the media coverage of the CFCs' high profits may also increase public sensitivity about the lenders' lack of morality. In the following subsection we analyze the press coverage for the *sarakin mondai* to emphasize the evolution of the public interest and its perception of the problem.

4.1. Press coverage analysis- methodology[30] and results

We analyzed the press coverage for the *sarakin mondai* from 1977 to 2006 by selecting articles from Asahi shinbun and Nikkei shinbun. We performed a search using the key word 'sarakin' and obtained more than 4000 articles. We chose to keep the term 'sarakin' instead of consumer finance (*shôhisha kinyû*) as 'sarakin' describes the reality of moneylenders' abusive practices.[31]

We found that political salience was high during each period that was marked by scandals related to the *sarakin* and that the government usually reacted by lowering the ceiling on interest rates, except in 2004 (Predatory Lending Act, which did not include a revision of the ceiling on interest rates)[32] (see Figure 4).

However, this apparently high level of political salience does not explain why the government did not regulate the market in favor of better borrowers' protection until 2006. In order to understand the subjects covered by the *Asahi Shinbun*, we have sorted the articles into sub-categories (see Figure 5).

(1) The category 'short news items' includes all articles covering issues of crimes, frauds, and hold-ups related to borrowers who have taken credits from sarakin.
(2) The category 'laws and regulation' includes all articles covering topics related to the legislative and regulatory processes including political and financial collusion between political parties and *sarakin.*
(3) The category 'civil society actions' includes all articles covering a broad range of topics related to over-indebtedness, personal bankruptcy and collective actions organized by borrowers' defense groups based on legal expertise. These actions increased during the 1990s in response to the rising number of scandals involving moneylenders (CFCs, small lenders, *shôkôron*, etc.).
(4) The category 'consumer credit market' includes all articles covering issues of CFCs business model, growth strategy, etc.

During the initial period of enactment of the Money Lending Business Act (1978–1984), the number of articles covering over-indebtedness as a social issue and civil society actions in defense of borrowers was low compared with the

Figure 4 Evolution of *sarakin mondai's salience*
Source: Data collection by the author from Asahi shinbun 1977–2006

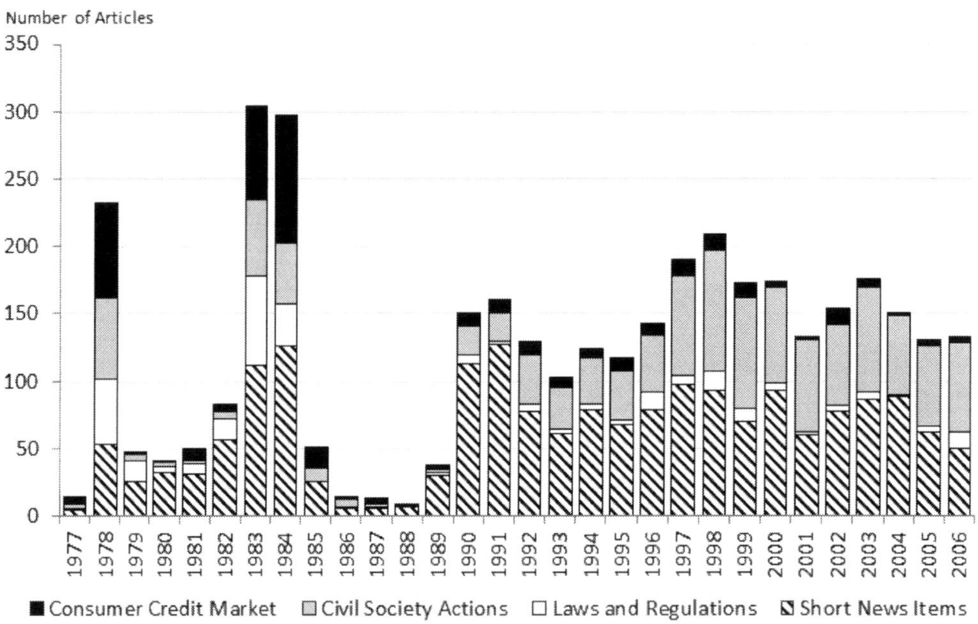

Figure 5 Analysis of the salience for *sarakin mondai* by sub-categories
Source: Data collection by the author from Asahi shinbun 1977–2006

number of articles covering the burning issues of borrowers' crime, fraud, and hold-ups. We can deduce from this analysis that general concern about the problem of over-indebtedness was low in the late 1970s to the 1990s. The newspaper nature of coverage of the issues related to *sarakin* had also nourished a negative perception of indebted borrowers among public opinion.

This low level of interest from journalists regarding the problems of over-indebtedness and personal bankruptcy may be explained by the economic context of stable growth until the mid-1980s, followed by the bubble economy (1989–1991), the maintenance of a high rate of saving and the accumulation of wealth by Japanese households (Horioka 2012). Personal bankruptcy was seen as an individual problem caused by over-borrowing, attributable to hedonistic behavior on the part of irresponsible consumers.[33] The public did not see personal bankruptcy and over-indebtedness as social issues of general concern. This low perception of the public opinion is also due to the lack of impact of borrowers' advocates to voice their interests in institutional arenas. During the 1970s and the 1980s, local consumer associations and groups of attorneys did not have sufficient experience and knowledge to organize and mobilize the defense and representation of the borrowers' diffuse interests. As we can see in Figure 6, the newspapers coverage of social issues related to *sarakin* was low, apart from a period during which the implementation of the Moneylenders Law was on the political agenda, in 1978 and then in 1983–1984.

Utsunomiya Kenji, one of the leaders of the group of lawyers, who organized the defense of borrowers and victims of predatory lending in the early 1980s, pointed out that Japanese lawyers were lacking the experience and training needed to defend consumers in general, and borrowers in particular.[34] This was partly due to the low level of consumer protection rights as mentioned by Kimura Tatsuya, another lawyer involved in the movement against *sarakin*'s abusive lending practices.[35] Utsunomiya also highlighted the fact that, as many lenders were linked to the Japanese mafia (*bôryokudan*), articles about the *sarakin* were widely diffused by the media as a result of the great number of scandals. Although this aspect of the market represented an obstacle to civil society in its effort to mobilize consumer defense, at the same time the high media coverage helped lawyers to communicate more easily through the newspapers about their actions to prevent borrowers from falling victim to illicit practices, and thus becoming over-indebted.[36] However, as our research shows, the newspaper coverage of these topics was very irregular until the end of the 1980s, reflecting low interest in the public opinion.

4.2. *Collective actions organized by groups of lawyers*

After the bubble burst, borrowers' defense groups composed of local consumers associations, local bar associations, as well as lawyers from the *Nichibenren* began

Figure 6 Articles in the category 'civil society action' sorted into two sub-categories
Source: Data collection by the author from Asahi shinbun 1977–1990

to better structure their actions at the local and national levels in response to the first significant increase of over-indebtedness and personal bankruptcy caused by over-borrowing (mainly due to credit cards) following the bubble period. By the 1990s, they provided more and more counseling and legal support at the local level, and organized several series of seminars and conferences to mobilize and inform the public about the risk of over-indebtedness, moneylenders' illicit practices and the options for legal recourse available to protect debtors from harsh collection practices. In Figures 7 and 8 we have sorted all articles related to civil society action and crimes. We observe a decreasing number of articles listed in the category of crimes related to *sarakin* and, on the contrary, an increasing number of articles listed in the category of civil society actions that might reflect a rising impact of borrowers' defense groups' collective actions. This rising number of articles related to civil society actions also shed light on the possible influence of lawyers over the judiciary power when defending borrowers' cases in courts. Since 2003, judicial power progressively decided to protect more systematically the borrowers.

Between 1996 and 2004, the government passed the Personal Bankruptcy Law's reform to ease the process of insolvency declaration. This reform helped

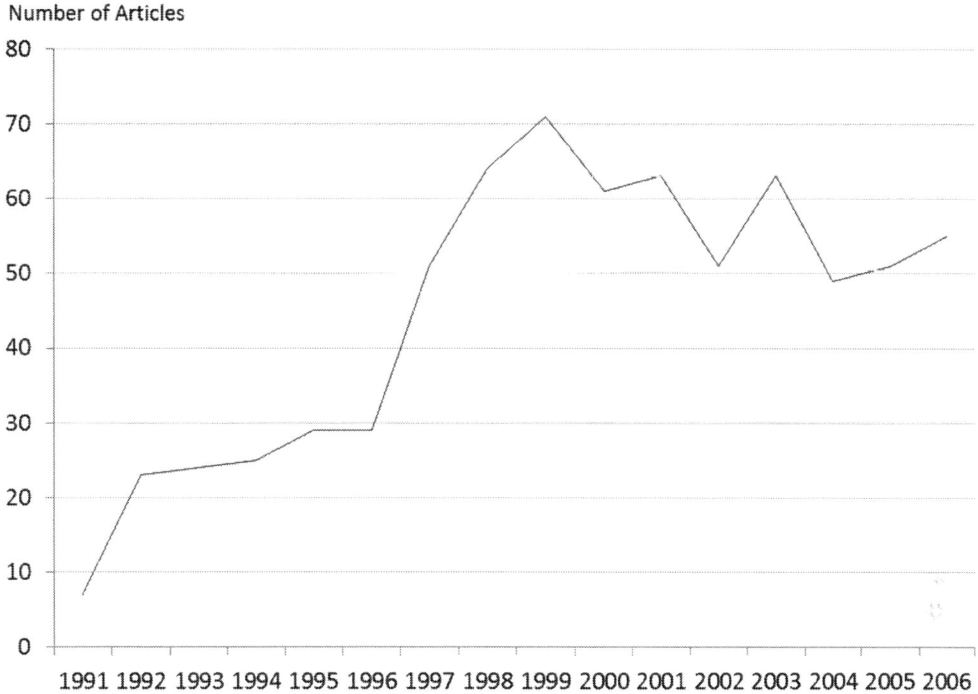

Figure 7 Articles from the Civil Society Actions category (1991–2006)
Source: Data collection by the author from Asahi Shinbun 1991–2006

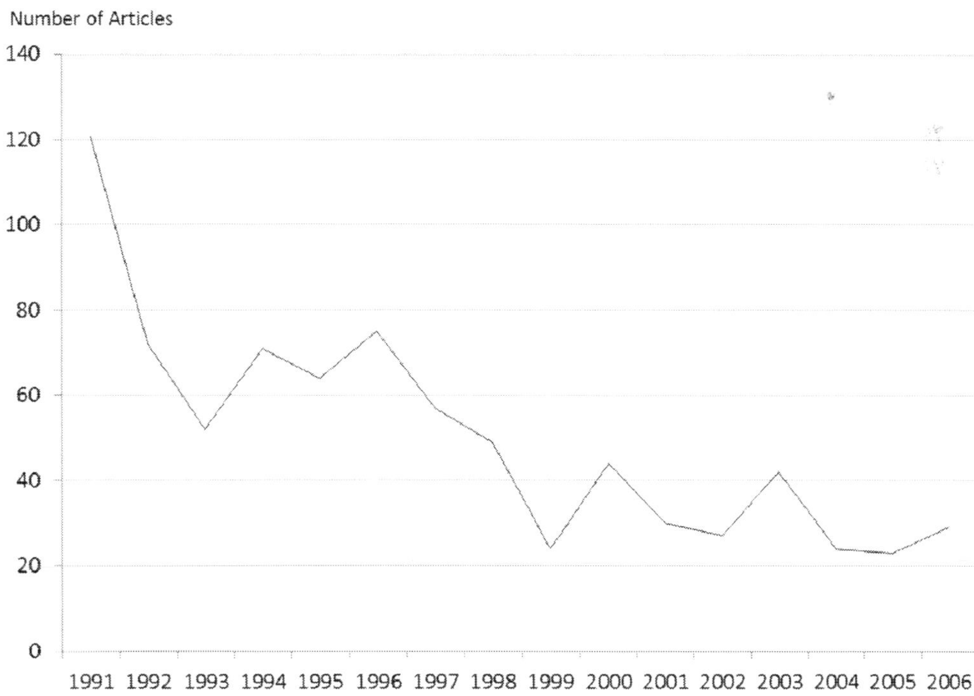

Figure 8 Articles from the Crime category (1991–2006)
Source: Data collection by the author from Asahi Shinbun 1991–2006

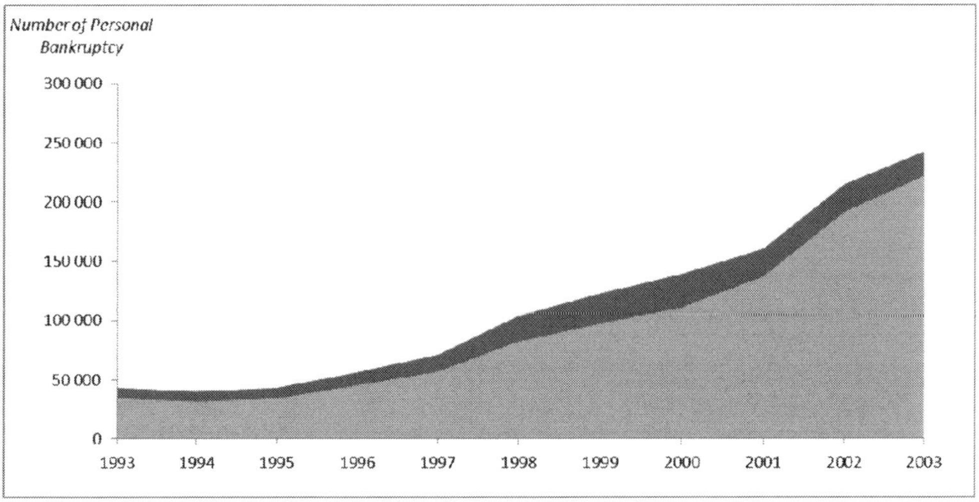

Figure 9 Number of personal bankruptcies caused by over-borrowing in the unsecured personal loan sector out of the total number of personal bankruptcy declarations
Source: Compilation of data from the Supreme Court (saikôsaibanjo - shihô tôkei nenpô) *in* Higuchi & Banno 2004

lawyers to defend over-indebted individuals. During the 1990s and the early 2000s, the number of over-borrowing consumers grew. Data on Japanese bankruptcy filings reflect the growing financial vulnerability of households at the bottom of the income ladder. These data show that the increased rate of bankruptcy filings was mainly due to over-borrowing on the unsecured loan market (see Figure 9).[37] Borrowers' defense groups pointed out that illicit practices and excess lending mainly caused the rising number of individuals filing for personal bankruptcy.

The increase in the number of articles covering those social issues was also the result of the Courts' series of decisions since 2005, especially the Supreme Court's final decision in January 2006, putting an end to the gray zone lending, which meant that borrowers could claim a refund for excess interest charges. This is known as a '*kabarai*' claim (see Figure 10).

Scholars at the Waseda University Institute for Research in Consumer Financial Services pointed out, in a survey on the rise of personal bankruptcy filings, that the problem was not caused directly by over-borrowing or by high interest rates, but rather because of economic reasons such as lower wages, and unexpected events such as job loss or health issues (Higuchi & Banno 2004). These results are consistent with other studies published on the problem in the USA. For example, M. White argues that the rise in the number of bankruptcy filings is less a question of financial deregulation than of an economic downturn leading to job loss, lower income and, thus, a heavier burden of debt (White 2007b). She also mentions the case of individual company and

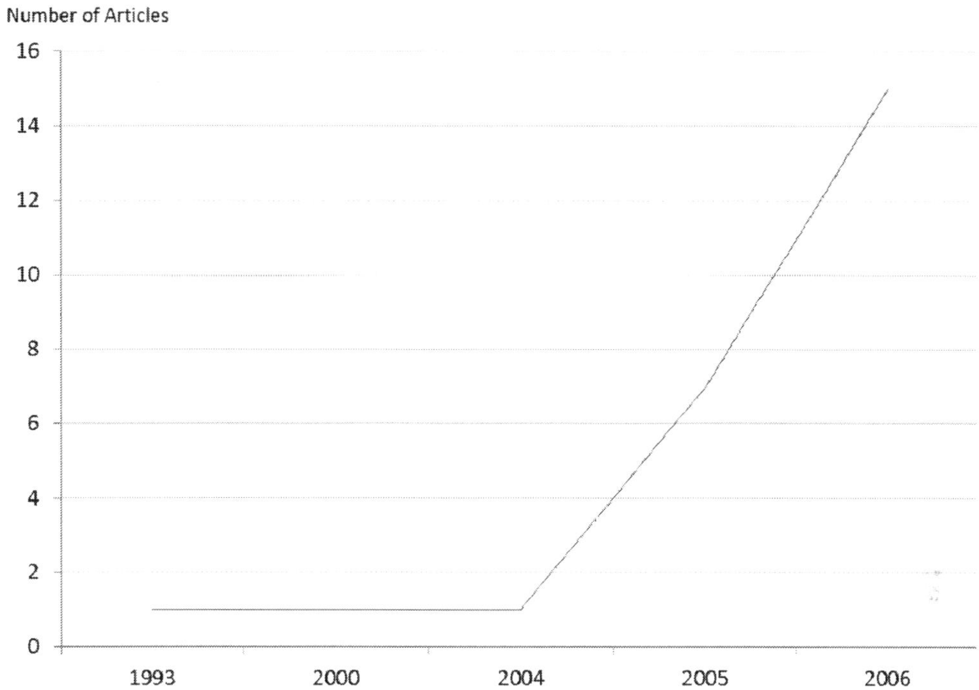

Figure 10 Increasing number of articles about people filing suit
Source: Data collection by the author from Asahi Shinbun 1991–2006

small business owners who suffered greatly during the economic crisis and eventually declared personal bankruptcy. In France as well, the government has recognized, since 2003, the problem of *passive indebtedness* (*surendettement passif*) due to unexpected events such as job loss, bad health or divorce, making the borrower unable to reimburse his or her loan (Gloukoviezoff 2009). In Japan, we observe that borrowers' defense groups led by highly popular personalities such as Utsunomiya Kenji, who became a political entrepreneur at the head of the movement for *sarakin* victims, incorporated their political discourse into a broader context of rising inequality (*kakusa shakai*), increasing poverty and the phenomenon of the *working poor.*[38] The *kabarai* procedure implemented by the Supreme Court allowed many indebted people to temporarily escape their debt.

4.3. *The new law of regulation (kasei kashikingyô hô) and its limits*

In 2006–2010, the government revised its policy for protecting consumers. This protection included measures to ensure transparency in consumer credit contracts, to limit excessive or extortionate lending and to ensure better collection and distribution of consumer credit histories, including the centralization of data, and better control over the privacy of personal data. On one hand, since 2010, Japan's regulations regarding consumer debtors provide a high level of protection across four areas: restrictions on credit advertising, borrowers' rights in contracting (usury cap) and repayment, recourse in case of over-indebtedness, and protection of private financial data, although the establishment of a positive data center for better access to credit is still only under consideration. On the other hand, the full implementation of the revised Money Lending Business Law in 2010 worries academic scholars. As a result of the legal amendments, consumer finance companies have tightened their credit standards for high-risk borrowers and a significant portion of borrowers are excluded from the market, including SMEs. (Domoto 2014) points out that regulating interest rates has evident side-effects as access to credit is reduced and causes borrowers who are considered high-risk (small business owners, temporary workers, etc.) to be excluded from the market. He observes that the new regulation resulted in an increase of informal loans (family loans and requests for loans on the black market). He also points out the lack of credit counseling services for those who are in difficulty from over-borrowing. Indeed the *kabarai* provision helps those who are heavily indebted in the short term but cannot solve the general problem of over-indebtedness. He argues that lawyers and judicial scriveners have a virtual monopoly in the area of debt adjustment; in a *kabarai* claim they receive a contingency fee of 20 to 30 per cent of the amount recovered from the moneylenders, encouraging attorneys and other legal professionals to continue to offer *kabarai* claim services (Domoto 2014). Following the Supreme Court decision, the seven major CFCs returned almost 1.6 trillion yen and 400 billion of this may well represent the amount received by the attorneys (Ramseyer 2013). Most of the CFCs went bankrupt. Attorneys and legal professionals who deal with debt adjustment made huge profits as the number of *kabarai* claims increased from 2006.[39]

5. Conclusion

In this article we have analyzed the changes that gradually transformed Japanese moneylenders business since the 1970s to the 2000s by focusing on the gap between the formal rules and informal practices of lenders that led to an excess of lending, abusive and illicit practices as well as over-borrowing and, in the worst cases, debt-related suicides. Our results are as follows. First, the revision of the Moneylenders Business Law (2006–2010) is the result of an accumulation of collective actions organized by lawyers to defend borrowers' interests, covered by the media and sustained by the judiciary power, as over-indebtedness became a subject of general concern in a period of economic downturn, an awareness of rising inequality (*kakusa shakai*) and growing poverty, resulting from greater economic insecurity. The media coverage of several scandals related to moneylenders and CFCs' abusive practices also changed the public's perception of social issues related to *sarakin mondai*.

This re-regulation is also the result of gradual institutional changes over a period of 30 years, highlighting a shift in power relations such that the groups of lawyers who were not involved in the original design of the law in the late 1970s to early 1980s, then they took it over and turned it to new ends (Streeck & Thelen 2005). Indeed, by relying on the *kabarai* procedure, lawyers helped indebted or liquidity-constrained individuals to gain access to liquidity in the short term. As Ramseyer (2013) argues, lawyers and judicial scriveners won a virtual monopoly in the area of debt adjustment and made huge profits with this new business. The growing legal experience of lawyers to defend borrowers as well as consumers, in general allows them to increase their influence in the legislative arena. It also reveals a greater capacity for civil society to organize the provision of better *weak interests* legal protection. But we also observe that lawyers' collective actions did not contribute to promoting social change.

In fact, the group of lawyers argued that over-borrowing was mainly due to unsecured credit lenders' illicit practices. Their arguments have focused on the major CFCs, which have made large profits by charging high interest rates. As a result, the public was more concerned about the lack of morality and justice in the sector than about the structural factors of the increasing financial vulnerability of lower income households, irregular workers, small business and VSEs.

Finally, the new regulation has radically modified the complementarity between bank and non-bank sectors by putting out of the market almost all lenders (first the small lenders, followed by the large CFCs). However, moneylenders assumed historically a social and economic function by providing loans to high-risk borrowers, mainly small business. Since the mid-2000s, commercial banks have entered the consumer finance market through acquisition of the large CFCs, but they don't provide small loans to high-risk borrowers such as small businesses and consumers, unlike many moneylenders who used to do it at the local level. This lack of efficiency of the credit sector to adapt to the characteristics of the Japanese economy and its financial system reveals the limit of the new law, which was mostly a response to a historical contradictory conflict of interests between two social groups over a profitable business: the loan business followed by the debt adjustment business.

In our current research, we are now focusing our attention on analyzing the dynamic that would explain the discrepancies between the moral objective of a cooperation between *weak interest* and lawyers, and the outcomes in term of new business opportunities supported by political parties, as well as a new type of collective action and its efficiency in bringing about social change or not. For example, the judiciary procedure – *kabarai* – was also used as a measure of social policy's substitution by the government to solve the problem of rising over-indebtedness in the short term. It seems that the coalition of interests between moneylenders and dominant political parties has changed in favor of the group of lawyers whose political influence has increased since the mid-2000s.

Acknowledgements

This research was generously supported by the Foundation France-Japon de l'EHESS and the Japan Foundation. I would like to thank Sébastien Lechevalier, David Chiavacci, Domoto Hiroshi, Kikkawa Takeo and Sebastian Bourgue; two anonymous readers also offered their detailed insights, for which I am most grateful. All errors are my responsibility alone.

Disclosure statement

No potential conflict of interest was reported by the author.

Funding

Fondation France-Japon de l'EHESS; European Union's Horizon 2020 research and innovation programme, Marie Skłodowska-Curie Grant No 645763.

Notes

1. Hyman (2011); Entreprise & Histoire (2010); *The Development of Consumer Credit in Global Perspective, Business, Regulation, and Culture, Worlds of Consumption* , Edited by Jan Logemann, Palgrave Macmillan, 2012; G. Bertola, R. Disney, C. Grant (2006) *The Economics of Consumer Credit*, Cambridge, MA: MIT Press; Niemi et al. (2009); Warren and Sullivan, *The fragile middle-class : American in debt*, Yale University Press, 2001; Trumbull (2014); David Kraft (2007) Private Law Control of Consumer Credit in the United Kingdom. *In*: Christian Twigg-Flessner et al., eds. *Yearbook of Consumer Law 2008* (Ashgate, 2007) 403.
2. Hayashi, F. (1986), *Why Is Japan's Saving Rate So Apparently High? In*: Stanley Fischer, ed., *NBER Macroeconomics Annual, vol. 1*, Cambridge, MA: MIT Press; Horioka, C.Y. (1993) Consuming and Saving. *In*: Andrew Gordon, ed. *Postwar Japan as History*, Berkeley: University of California Press; Horioka, C.Y. (1995) Is Japan's Household Saving Rate Really High? *Review of Income and Wealth*, 41(4); Ronald, M.J. (2002) Credit Cards and Debit Cards in the United States and Japan, *Vanderbit Law Review*, 5.
3. Nomura Japanese Economic Research (November, 2002) https://www.nri.com/global/news/2002/021119/021119.pdf (BOJ, Flow of funds / and Family Income and Expenditure Survey)
4. Japan Federation of Bar Associations (Nichibenren) reports available for 1994, 1997, 2002
5. Although the CFCs objected to many of the measures proposed by the government regulatory policies, such as the ceiling on interest rates, it seems that they were excluded from the policy process (Trumbull 2012)
6. Article Asahi 13 May 1972.
7. Article Asahi 13 October 1978.
8. The IRRA capped maximum interest rates at 20 per cent, depending on the amount of the principal, although article 1 mentions that 'The agreement on interest shall be null and void with regard to the portion which is in excess'. Paragraph 2, however, states: 'Where the debtor has voluntarily paid a portion in excess... he may not demand the refund thereof...', thus leaving plenty of room for 'voluntary payment'; Pardieck (2008). This practice was strongly criticized by the judiciary power since the Supreme Court rulings in 1964 and 1968.
9. Nikkei article 21 March 1983; Asahi article 30 April 1983.

10. *Kashikingyô no kisei nado ni kansuru hôritsu* (The Money Lending Industry Regulation Act, Law No. 32, 1983) http://law.e-gov.go.jp/htmldata/S58/S58HO032.html
11. Asahi shinbun Article 15 June 1978; Article 17 June 1978; Article 1 September 1983; article 2 September 1983; article 20 October 1983; 4 September 1984; 12 November 1984.
12. *Shôhisha shinyô no arikata ni tsuite – kinyûseidô chôkai senmon iinkai hôkoku*, zaikei shôhosha, 1987.
13. OECD Economic Outlook, no. 54 (December 1993) in Horioka (2012).
14. Article Nikkei 10 November 1984.
15. Article Asahi 9 October 1991; Article Asahi 17 October 1991; Article Asahi 20 October 1991.
16. During the 1970s and 1980s, CFCs experienced difficulties in raising funds as a result of the negative image associated with moneylending. In addition, at the beginning of the 1980s, banks and CFCs had diverging interests on the consumer finance market, as banks started to show their willingness to enter this profitable sector. The MoF sent several informal warnings (*tsutatsu*) to the banking sector requesting them to lower interest rates on their loans to the CFCs.
17. Promise Co, Ltd, Annual report, 1996, 1997, 1998, 1999, 2000.
18. Acom Co. Ltd, Aiful Co. Ltd, Promise Co, Ltd, Annual Report, 1999, 2000.
19. Kamata S. (2005) Les classes fortunées au Japon de Meiji à nos jours. *In*: Saint Simon, ed. *La dynamique du Japon, sous la direction de Jean-François Sabouret.*
20. In 2004, bank financing still represented the major source of funding for the major CFCs. Promise had strong financial ties with the Long-Term Credit Bank of Japan, Sumitomo Trust and Banking (Promise Co, Ltd. Annual Report, 2005).
21. Acom Co. Ltd, Aiful Co. Ltd, Promise Co, Ltd, Annual Report, 1996,1997; 1998; 1999, 2000, 2001, 2002.
22. *Ibid.*
23. Kigaruni ni narenu sarakin CM, 8 January2002, Asahi Shinbun; 'Sarakin CM' an-isanaika, (koe) 11 January 2002, Asahi Shinbun.
24. *Annual reports of the Japan Consumer Credit Association.*
25. Matsushita J. (2006) Comprehensive Reform of Japanese Personal Insolvency Law. *Theoretical Inquiries in Law* 7(2).
26. See Pardieck (2008).
27. The lack of security and control is a problem not only for the unsecured credit market: the credit card market expansion, which began in the mid-1990s, is also suffering from an increase of frauds related to the low payment system.
28. The consumer credit market is divided up between the different types of lenders: installment sales companies (Shinpan) are under METI control, while credit card companies, CFCs and banks are under MoF control. Because of the segmentation of the consumer credit market there is no centralized database. The lack of shared information about borrowers' credit histories results in excessive lending.
29. Japan Federation of Bar Associations (Nichibenren) reports available for 1994, 1997, 2002, 2005 and 2008.
30. We conducted this research in Tokyo from 2012 to 2013. We used newspapers, Asahi and Nikkei database. We built a database with all the articles listed by category depending on the topics and theme of the article, but also the number of words and its visibility. This research helps us to bypass the main difficulty of our research subject, which was the access to relevant sources that cover the entire period.
31. The major CFCs (Promise, Takefuji, Aiful, Acom) initiated legal proceedings against Asahi Shinbun for using the term 'sarakin' instead of 'shôhisha kinyu'.
32. In 1978, scandals occurred and forced the government to pass a regulation in 1983; in 1991 the bubble burst and government lowered the ceiling on interest rates to 40.0004 per cent; in 1998, as a result of *shôkôron mondai*, the government lowered the ceiling on interest rates to 29.2 per cent; in 2003, the *yamikin* scandals occurred.

33. Interview of a Kimura, a lawyer leader of the movement against *sarakin*, predatory lending: http://blog.livedoor.jp/bengoshiretsuden/archives/51321341.html
34. Utsunomiya Kenji' homepage at http://utsunomiyakenji.com/what/
35. Article 29 April 1978; Article Nikkei 27 November 1995.
36. Utsunomiya Kenji' homepage at http://utsunomiyakenji.com/what/
37. These data are compiled by the Japan Federation of Bar Associations (Nichibenren) in reports available for 1994, 1997, 2002, 2005 and 2008: data for 2005: number of personal bankruptcy filings: 184,000; number of borrowers from *sarakin*: 14,000,000; number of borrowers from more than five lenders: 2,300,000; number of suicides due to economic and financial vulnerability: 7800. Source: Nichibenren report, 2006.
38. Kondankai (study group 2005–2006) Utsunomiya Kenji's intervention, session 2 – 27 April 2005 available at http://www.fsa.go.jp/singi/singi_kasikin/singi_kasikin.html
39. General Electric finalizes exit from Japanese consumer Finance, 26 February 2014, *Financial Times*; This is very similar to what happened in the UK in the early 1990s, when the IVA (Individual Voluntary Agreement) became a popular alternative for over-indebted household consumers who hoped to avoid a formal bankruptcy proceeding. The UK consumer debt management companies, which arranged IVAs for a percentage-based fee, made significant profits and began to promote their services in fairly aggressive marketing campaigns (Trumbull 2012).

References

Arthur, J. and Alexander, K.D.O., 1989. *The development and structure of consumer credit in Japan*. Santa-Monica: Rand note publication series.

Baron, D.P., 1994. Electoral competition with informed and uninformed voters. *American Political Science Review*, 88(01), 33–47.

Calder, K., 1988. *Crisis and compensation: public policy and political stability in Japan, 1949-1986*. Princeton: Princeton University Press.

Calder, L., 1999. *Financing the American dream: a cultural history of consumer credit*. Princeton University Press.

Culpepper, P.D., 2010. *Quiet politics and business power: corporate control in Europe and Japan*. Cambridge: Cambridge University Press.

Domoto, H., 2014. *Kasei kashikingyôhô ga manuita fukusaiyô ni kansuru kenshô. Pa-sonaru fainansu kenkyû*, Pa-sonaru fainansu gakkai (No. 1), 55–65.

Francks, P. and Hunter, J. eds., 2011. *The historical consumer: consumption and everyday life in Japan*, 1850–2000. London: Macmillan Palgrave UK.

Garon, S., 2011. *Beyond our means: Why America spends while the world savers*. Princeton: Princeton University Press.

Gelpi, E. and Labruyère, J., 1994. *Histoire du crédit à la consommation: doctrines et pratiques*. Paris: La Découverte.

Glickman, L.B. ed., 1999. *Consumer society in American history: a reader*. Ithaca, NY: Cornell University Press.

Gloukoviezoff, G., 2009. L'exclusion bancaire: de quoi parle-t-on? Une perspective française. *Vie & sciences de l'entreprise*, (2), 9–20.

Gordon, A., 2006. From singer to shinpan: consumer credit in modern Japan. In: *The ambivalent consumer: questioning consumption in East Asia and the West*. Ithaca, NY: Cornell University Press, 137–162.

Gordon, A., 2012. *Fabricating consumers: the sewing machine in modern Japan*. Berkeley, CA: University of California Press.

Graeber, D., 2014. *Debt-updated and expanded: the first 5,000 years*. Brooklyn: Melville House.

Higuchi, T. and Banno, T., 2004. *shôhisha kinyû kokyaku to jikohassan*. Tokyo: Institute For Research On Credit Business Waseda University.

Horioka, C.Y., 2012. *Are Japanese households financially healthy, and if so, why? A Group of Seven (G7) comparison*. ISER Discussion Paper, Institute of Social and Economic Research, Osaka University, No. 859.

Horioka, C. Y., 1990. Why is Japan's household saving rate so high? A literature survey. *Journal of the Japanese and International Economies*, 4(1), 49–92.

Hoshi, T. and Kashyap, A., 2001. *Corporate financing and corporate governance in Japan: the road to the future*. Boston: MIT Press.

Hyman, L., 2011. *Debtor nation: the history of America in red ink: the history of America in red ink*. Princeton: Princeton University Press.

Kobayashi, W. and Ono, T., 2010. *nihon no kakei chochiku ritsu*, Finance N4, Rapport special disponible. Available from: http://www.mof.go.jp/pri/research/special_report/f01_2010_04.pdf

Kollman, K., 1998. *Outside lobbying: public opinion and interest group strategies*. Princeton: Princeton University Press.

Kozuka, S. and Nottage, L.R., 2007. Re-regulating unsecured consumer credit in Japan: over-indebted borrowers, the supreme court, and new legislation. *Sydney Law School Research Paper*, No. 07/62.

Kozuka, S. and Nottage, L.R., 2009. *The myth of the cautious consumer: Law, culture, economics and politics in the rise and partial fall of unsecured lending in Japan*. Sidney: University of Sidney Legal Studies Research Paper, June.

Logemann, J., 2012. From cradle to bankruptcy? Credit access and the American welfare state. In: *The development of consumer credit in global perspective: business, regulation, and culture*. Palgrave Macmillan US, 201–219.

Maclachlan, P., 2002. *Consumer politics in postwar Japan: The institutional boundaries of citizen activism*. New York: Columbia University Press.

Niemi, J., I, R., and Whitforf, W.C., 2009. *Consumer credit, debt and bankruptcy, comparative and international perspectives*. Oxford: Hart Press Ed.

Olson, M., 1965. *The logic of collective action*. Cambridge, MA: Harvard University Press.

Pardieck, A., 2008. Japan and the moneylenders: activist courts and substantive justice. *Pacific Rim Law & Policy Journal*, 17, 529–568.

Partner, S., 2000. *Assembled in Japan: electrical goods and the making of the Japanese consumer*. Berkeley, CA: University of California Press.

Patterson, T.E., 1993. *Out of order: how the decline of the political parties and the growing power of the news media undermine the American way of electing presidents*. New York, NY: Alfred Knopf.

Posner, E.A., 1995. Contract law in the welfare state: a defense of the unconscionability doctrine, usury laws, and related limitations on the freedom to contract. *The Journal of Legal Studies*, 24 (2), 283–319.

Ramseyer, M., 2013. *Bottom-Feeding at the Bar: Usury law and value-dissipating attorneys in Japan*. Cambridge, MA: Harvard Law School.

Sala, A., 2015. Dette usurière et mouvements sociaux dans le Japon moderne (1868–1937). *Histoire et Mesure*, 30(1), 43–68.

Shibuya, R., 1972. *Shichiya taisaku rippô no tenkai* [Modification de la loi de réglementation appliquée aux prêteurs sur gage]. Komazawa: Komazawa daigaku keizai gakurônshû.

Shibuya, R., 2001. *Shominkinyû no tenkai to seisaku taiyô* [Evolution de la finance populaire et changement de politique]. Tokyo: Gakujutsu shuppankai.

Stigler, G.J., 1971. The theory of economic regulation. *The Bell Journal of Economics and Management Science*, 2(1), 3–21.

Streeck, W. and Thelen, K., 2005. *Beyond continuity: institutional change in advanced political economies*. Oxford: Oxford University Press.

Suda, S., 2006. *Karyugui—Shohisha Kinyu No Jittai*. Tokyo: Takuma Shinsho.
Sullivan, T.A, Warren, E., and Westbrook, J.L., 2000. *The fragile middle class: Americans in debt*. London: Yale University Press.
TAPALS (ed.), 2006. *Tapals Hakusho (Tapals White Paper)*. Tokyo: TAPALS (Shohisha Kinyu Renrakukai).
Trumbull, G., 2012. *Strength in numbers: the political power of weak interests*. Cambridge, MA: Harvard University Press.
Trumbull, G., 2014. *Consumer lending in France and America*. New York, NY: Cambridge University Press.
Utsunomiya, K., 2007. *tajûsaimu no tadashii kaiketsu hô, Kadensha* Tokyo.
West, M.D., 2005. *Law in everyday Japan: sex, sumo, suicide, and statutes*. Chicago: University of Chicago Press.
White, M.J., 2007a. Bankruptcy law. In: *Handbook of law and economics*; Vol. 2. Amsterdam: Elsevier, 1013–1072.
White, M.J., 2007b. Bankruptcy reform and credit cards. *The Journal of Economic Perspectives*, 21 (4), 175–199.
Wilson, J., 1973. *Political organization*. New York: Basic Book.
Wilson, J., 1980. *The politics of regulation*. New York: Basic Book.

Re-packaging old policies? 'Abenomics' and the lack of an alternative growth model for Japan's political economy

SAORI SHIBATA

Abstract: 'Abenomics' has continued to attract the attention of both the national and international media and a broad range of scholars. There are different and contested views of Abenomics and its impact upon the Japanese economy. This article argues that those more Keynesian-style remedies that form part of Abenomics have not been able to address Japan's longer-term problem of weak demand, especially in terms of private consumption. This is in large part due to the liberalising measures that also form part of Abenomics, and which are incompatible with the Keynesian remedies pursued. Whilst Abenomics has the potential (at least in the short-to-medium term) to improve the profitability of Japanese businesses, in the absence of a corresponding move to redistribute corporate wealth to labour, Abenomics also represents a hazard to future economic growth in Japan.

Introduction

Since Prime Minister Abe announced his strategy to revive Japan's economy in 2013 the term 'Abenomics' has continued to attract the attention of both the national and international media and a broad range of scholars. Discussions have tended to vary in terms of the degree of support voiced for Abenomics. Many of the early observations made in the national and international media were positive, noting especially the boost to stock prices and the depreciation of the yen. Evaluations have tended subsequently to divide into three groups. The first group of commentators have praised Abenomics, highlighting the effects of the expansionary monetary policy upon expected inflation, the resultant increase in stock prices and general increase in corporate profits, and the increased rate of employment and level of public consumption (IMF 2013, Hausman and Wieland 2014). A second group of commentators, whilst broadly supportive of Abenomics, have proposed a number of revisions, including the non-implementation of the planned consumption tax increase (Kataoka 2014, Takahashi 2014, Krugman 2014), the establishment of a fund for SMEs (Krugman 2014, Yoshino and Taghizadeh-Hesary 2014), the increase in the productivity of firms and investment in human capital and ICT capital (Fukao 2013), and/or much further implementation of liberalisation (Fukao 2013, Katz 2014, OECD 2015a). The third group, in contrast, have been more critical in their evaluation of Abenomics, focusing especially on the 'third arrow' – that is, Abe's longer-term structural reform strategy – emphasising the way in which the first and second arrows contribute to the expansion of corporate profit, whilst the third arrow will undermine and destabilise those most vulnerable within Japan's labour market and wider society. As such, Abenomics is depicted as a deepening of precarity and inequality within Japanese society (Ueda 2013, Wolf 2013, Ito 2014, Roberts 2014).

This article engages with the debate regarding the merits of Abenomics. It locates Abenomics within the historical transformation of Japan's socio-economic institutions. It goes on to examine the extent to which Abenomics has contributed to the growth or non-growth of Japan's economy, whether Abenomics represents an alternative growth model for the Japanese economy, and the key challenges that Abenomics faces. The article presents an overview of the historical transformation of Japan's political economy, arguing that Abenomics is a mix of both Keynesian and neoliberal remedies, the effects of which are both limited and not as unconventional as some commentators have emphasised (cf. Takahashi 2014, Hausman and Wieland 2014). Indeed, Abenomics is not distinctively different from the reforms of Abe's predecessors.

The article also takes issue with the aims of the so-called 'third arrow'; that is, Abe's neoliberal policy package. This, it is argued, poses a threat to the stability of Japan's economy, and especially to its workforce. Those more Keynesian-styled remedies that are included within Abenomics have therefore not sought to address Japan's longer-term problem of weak demand, especially in terms of private consumption. Whilst Abenomics has the potential (at least in the short-to-medium term) to improve the profitability of Japanese business, without witnessing a corresponding move to redistribute corporate wealth to labour, Abenomics also represents a hazard to future economic growth in Japan and therefore it appears unable to cure its underlying longer-term problems.

The article is divided into three parts, the first providing an overview of the historical transformation of Japan's political economy between the 1980s and 2000s. The second part introduces the views, narratives and current debates over Abenomics. The third section seeks to provide an analysis and examination of Abenomics in the context of the historical transformation of Japan's socio-economic institutions. The paper argues that Abenomics, which is a mix of

Keynesian remedies and liberalisation, fails to address the current problems of instability in the labour market in Japan, and the lack of adequate policies that can achieve a certain degree of compromise between the government/capital and labour may harm the potential benefits of Abenomics.

Coordination and liberalisation? The transformation of Japan's political economy between the 1980s and 2000s

The institutions that form the Japanese economy have experienced a significant level of change over the last 30 years. This includes the labour market, financial market, corporate governance, models of firms, the form of the Japanese state, and Japan's trade relations. Many refer to the bursting of the bubble economy in the early 1990s as a turning point in terms of change in the Japanese political economy (Vogel 2006, Boyer et al. 2012, Isogai 2012, Uemura 2012, Yamada and Hirano 2012, Fukao 2013, Lechevalier 2014, Schiff 2015). These commentators also highlight the significant changes witnessed in the Japanese economy. This section explains key socio-economic changes between the 1980s and 2000s, paying attention to the process of institutional transformation (especially those institutions that govern the capital–labour relations that constitute Japan's model of capitalism) in order to provide a context within which we can locate Abenomics.

Japanese capitalism has experienced a trajectory of liberalisation, combined with a decline in economic growth, an institutional crisis and a lack of coordination between institutions and between actors over the past thirty years (Lechevalier 2014, Tiberghien 2014). The institutional change has been remarkable and resulted in a trend of (neo-)liberalisation. The earlier 'classic' Japanese system was characterised by coordination and a certain degree of consensus. Coordination in Japan's political economy had benefits and limits. Benefits included the diffusion of technical and organisation innovations. For instance, in the case of Toyotism (Boyer et al. 1998, cited in Lechevalier 2014, p. 7), the specific mode of production was spread to group-firms and firms in other countries. Moreover, coordination acted to reduce fluctuations in a firm's profits as well as at the macroeconomic level (Lechevalier 2014, p. 7). Similarly, networks between firms and between firms and banks enabled many firms to share information, risk, and sustain long-term relations. This type of coordination can act to stabilise production and capital-labour relations, leading to less fluctuations in a firm's profits and employment status (Hall and Sosckice 2001).

Coordination in the classic Japanese economic model also allowed for negotiated outcomes that acted to limit the growth of inequality (Lechevalier 2014, p. 7). For instance, the Japanese labour market witnessed an eradication of industrial unions and a move toward more cooperative union leaders and enterprise unions – a process that was complete by around the time of the 1970s (Jeong and Aguilera 2008, p. 119). In this type of coordinated labour market, capital and labour regularly acted to form compromises, to a greater extent than in more free market economies. Indeed, one of the trademarks of the post-war Japanese model of capitalism is the prevalence of long-term employment (Estévez-Abe 2008, p. 171), which provided social security (Schaede 2004, p. 283). The government set up this policy through a series of court decisions that made it almost impossible for a company to lay off workers (Schaede 2004, p. 283). As a result, by the 1970s long-term employment had become an institutionalised system underpinned by employment legislation (Schaede 2004, p. 283). Japan's labour market therefore used to be characterised by its stability, including long-term relations between employers and employees, a seniority-based wage system, and enterprise unionism that enabled relatively stable capital-labour relations (Rebick 2005, Witt 2006, Weathers 2008, Imai 2011, Lechevalier 2014, Tiberghien 2014, Uemura and Tahara 2014). This is not to say that all labour relations were harmonious, but discontent among workers was pacified to a considerable extent.

Moreover, the role of the state contributed to the degree of coordination that marked Japan's classic economic model. The level of deregulation and liberalisation in the market, which can be affected by the state has a significant impact upon the type of market economy. In the case of Japan, the state is generally considered to intervene in the market more than it does in more liberal market economies. This model of the Japanese state developed during the post-war period and leading up until the 1980s, and was commonly termed a developmental state. Until the mid-1970s, the Japanese government protected key domestic manufacturers from international competition by adopting a high wall of import tariffs (Rosenbluth and Thies 2010, p. 83). The state also used its public spending and increased labour demand to support core industries, including the construction industry, providing employment opportunities (Estévez-Abe 2008, p. 186). The Japanese state played a significant role in terms of the coordination of institutions and negotiation in the market.

However, coordination, which characterised 'classic' Japanese capitalism, has been continuously challenged from the late 1980s onwards following the entry of the Japanese economy into a period of slow growth. Having experienced over-accumulation, Japanese capital sought to restructure its mode of production in order to increase the rate of profit. This was accompanied by a process of deindustrialisation from the 1990s onward, whereby we witnessed a shift from manufacturing to the service industry (Uemura and Tahara 2014). This trend of deindustrialisation also advanced the process of flexibilisation of labour, as it saw the expansion of the proportion of non-regular workers in the labour force. This was therefore a key change in capital–labour relations in Japan, as stability and long-term relations were (and continue to be) weakened significantly.

Along with the change in industrial structure and Japan's slow economic growth, the role of the state in terms of its coordinating role within Japan's economy also changed from the late 1980s onwards. That is, the state took an active role in promoting flexibilisation within the labour market. The introduction of the Worker Dispatching Law in 1985 was a key initial trigger for the flexibilisation and casualisation of labour in Japan. This law was launched by the Nakasone government (1982–1986), in order to deregulate and liberalise the Japanese labour market as a part of a project of neoliberalisation. Similarly, the Koizumi-led government (2001–2006) took a lead in accelerating the process of neoliberalisation in the labour market. It also revised the Worker Dispatching Law in 2003, and the Labour Standard Law in 2004, and shifted risks inherent to employment liberalisation onto non-regular workers whilst preserving employment security for regular workers (Yun 2010, pp. 5,9). The amendment of the Labour Standard Law in 2004 also saw an additional clause being adopted, which recognised employers' right to dismissal (Vogel 2006, p. 81, Yun 2010, p. 12). This amendment also weakened the level of stability in capital-labour relations, making the Japanese labour market ever more unstable, especially for non-regular workers.

When this amendment was proposed in the advisory council, *Rengo*, the leading national unions' association, and union representatives, were unable to exercise a veto because of divisions between the unions on this issue (Hamaguchi 2003, cited in Watanabe 2012, p. 29). Some labour unions opposed deregulation, whereas others in the automotive and electronics industries (which possessed an influential position in *Rengo*) welcomed the proposal (Hamaguchi 2003, cited in Watanabe 2012, p. 29). This amendment further enhanced the flexibility of employment practices facing non-regular workers, without introducing appropriate protections for them. These amendments, introduced in the early 2000s, consolidated existing inequalities between regular and non-regular workers (Yun 2010, p. 9). The Koizumi Government reduced employment protection for non-regular workers whilst preserving it for core regular workers (Vogel 2006, p. 81). It visibly favoured capital over labour, heightening social tensions and class antagonism. This represented a significant change to the way in which negotiation and coordination had been conducted by the Japanese state.

This change was accelerated further still in the late 2000s. Non-regular workers have experienced an exacerbation of their precarious employment status in the aftermath of the Global Financial Crisis, as well as following the Fukushima disaster in March 2011. Many firms conducted large-scale dismissals of non-regular workers after the 2007–2008 financial crisis as well as small-scale but frequent dismissals of non-regular workers. For instance, 270,000 non-regular workers lost their jobs during this period due to either dismissals before their contracts expired or to the termination of contracts (Ministry of Health, Labour and Welfare 2010, p. 16). Between 2007 and 2009, involuntary job losses reached 790,000 (compared with only 480,000 dismissals during the Asian Financial Crisis of 1997–1999, and 490,000 between 2000 and 2003) (Ministry of Health, Labour and Welfare 2010, p. 14). Workers had to pay the cost of worsened business conditions, as employers exerted their domination over employees. The long-term unemployment rate (the ratio of the unemployed over one year amongst the unemployed) hit its record-high of 38.7 per cent in 2011 in the aftermath of the Fukushima disaster (Ministry of Health, Labour and Welfare 2013, p. 9). Corporate elites adopted numerous measures to cut labour costs and restructure capital–labour relations, reasserting their dominance and authority over the working class. Labour has therefore been placed in a more precarious and impoverished status, demonstrating the increasingly antagonistic nature of capital–labour relations in Japan (Shibata 2016).

Japanese capitalism has therefore experienced stagnation since the bursting of its bubble economy, driving firms to restructure in order to regain profit rates and productivity. This has also triggered flexibilisation of labour markets and has been destabilising long-term capital–labour relations. The Japanese government has also changed its role in the sense that it intervened in the market to liberalise and deregulate in favour of capital. The level of coordination and negotiation in the Japanese model of capitalism has therefore been undermined from the late 1980s onwards. This article now examines how the current project of Abenomics fits within this broader transformation of Japanese capitalism.

Abenomics: contested economic policies

Abenomics, since its start in 2013, has attracted much attention. The effects of Abenomics, particularly its monetary and fiscal policies, have been debated frequently among many commentators (see for instance, Krugman 2013, Ueda 2013, Fujiwara et al. 2014, Hausman and Wieland 2014, Yoshino and Taghizadeh-Hesary 2014, Roberts 2014, 2015, Takahashi 2014, Schiff 2015). This section will introduce the so-called 'three arrows' of Abenomics and the debates that have been engaged in on the topic. It will also examine how Abenomics contributes to Japan's current economic model and seek to explain the preliminary effects of Abenomics upon the Japanese economy.

Bold monetary policy (the first arrow)

The first arrow of Abenomics was launched in 2013 as a form of 'quantitative and qualitative easing' (QQE) in order to increase the monetary base in the Japanese market (Cabinet Office 2014b; Fujiwara et al. 2014). In this sense, monetary policy is being used according to Keynesian prescriptions, viewed as a necessary remedy during economic recession (see, for instance, Krugman 2013). The bold monetary policy here refers to the increase in the monetary base by the Bank of Japan through its 'quantitative easing, forward guidance of interest rates, and/or future asset purchases' (Ueda 2013, p. 253). PM Abe also instructed the Bank of Japan (BOJ) to increase its inflation target to 2 per cent and engage in unlimited easing (Hausman and Wieland 2014, p. 2).

The success of quantitative easing depends on whether this can change expectations of markets and induce change in agents' perceptions of monetary policy (Fujiwara, et al. 2014, p. 4). As soon as the announcement of the monetary policy package was made on 4 April, JGB yields rose, stock prices increased (by 20 per cent in early June) and the Japanese yen depreciated against the dollar by 10 per cent (Ueda 2013, p. 263). We also witnessed an increase in GDP in 2013 to an annualised rate of 3 per cent on a quarter-on-quarter basis, an improvement in exports due to the yen's depreciation, and an increase in the CPI (consumer price index) from negative to over 1 per cent (Uchida 2014, p. 249). However, the main benefits of the widely praised monetary policy, namely the increase in stock prices, have been led by foreign investors via their aggressive buying of Japanese stocks and selling of Japanese yen, not by domestic investors (Ito 2014, p. 108, Katz 2014, Fukuda 2015). The limited level of domestic investors' participation thus also implies that domestic investors remain sceptical about the effects of Abenomics.

Moreover, the BOJ Governor Kuroda's announcement of his intention to increase inflation to 2 per cent in two years temporarily triggered an increase in consumer prices (up by 1.3 per cent from the previous year). Hausman and Wieland (2014) argue that this monetary policy brought about the rapid growth of the broad money supply and changed expectations towards lower future real interest rates, resulting in increased credit demand, which further creates money in the banking system (Hausman and Wieland 2014, pp. 24–25). Due to this, the current monetary policy under Abenomics is viewed as different from previous experiments with monetary policies in 2001 and 2006 (Hausman and Wieland 2014, pp. 23–24). However, inflation expectations still remained around 1 per cent without much abrupt impact (Fujiwara et al. 2014, p. 6). This inflation is even considered to have occurred mainly due to a 25 per cent drop in the value of the Japanese yen, which raised prices on imports (Katz 2014). The impact of the monetary policy upon inflation seems to be modest. This is important because Kuroda's hope is that inflation would trigger more consumption and that this increase in spending would encourage firms to increase investment and therefore jobs (Ito 2014, Katz 2014).

Furthermore, this monetary policy initially increased the consumer confidence index from around 40 per cent in January 2013 to roughly 45 per cent in July 2013. However, this index dropped from 45 per cent to around 38 per cent in January 2015 (Cabinet Office 2015d). With a limited success in terms of inflation and due to a newly introduced tax hike in April 2014, the effect of monetary policy has been dampened, generating only modest change.

Reflecting the rise in stock prices and the depreciation of the Japanese yen, consumer spending initially 'pushed first quarter economic growth up 3.5 per cent annually and remained strong in the second quarter of 2013' (Fukuda 2015, p. 2). However, this new positive trend in the market did not last long as Japanese consumers appear to have acted contrary to expectations. Indeed, the data show that the expectation of price increases actually resulted in Japanese consumers spending less since the mid-2013, contrary to Kuroda's expectation (Katz 2014). This may not be so difficult to deduce from Japan's economic condition, whereby we have witnessed a decline in labour's share of income (Aoyagi and Ganeli 2015, p. 224) and only a small rise in wage among regular workers but a decrease for non-regular workers. For instance, the monthly wage of regular workers increased from 201,694 yen in 2012 to 404,720 yen in 2013, whereas that of non-regular workers decreased from 97,177 yen in 2012 to 96,644 yen in 2013 (Ministry of Health, Labour and Welfare 2014, p. 36, 2015). The wages of regular workers in May 2015 increased by 0.6 per cent in comparison with the previous year, whereas those of non-regular workers decreased by 0.7 per cent (Gekkan Kinrou Toukei Chousa May 2015), increasing the wage disparity between regular and non-regular workers. Further, we have not witnessed increases in secure and long-term jobs. As discussed above, the expansion of the number of non-regular workers under Abenomics has created a situation whereby an increasing number of workers engage in unstable employment with little chance of wage increases. This is a trend that has increased under the current LDP government (Ito 2014, pp. 103–107).

The positive evaluation of Abenomics turned into growing scepticism following the market crash on 23 May 2013 (Fukuda 2015, p. 2). Long-term inflation expectations have not risen substantially. Further, since the Japanese economy was close to a long-term liquidity trap, there was little room for further monetary policy accommodation (Fujiwara et al. 2014, p. 7). Moreover, the level of private investment in the first quarter of 2013 in all industries except the software sector has remained stagnant (the rates of investment growth have been between –0.4 and 0 percent during the FY2014) (Kataoka 2014, pp. 37–39, Oouchi and Ikuta 2015). The bold monetary policy (increased monetary base via the BOJ's large-scale purchase of the government bonds), however, has a limited effect on stimulating investment (Ohishi 2015, p. 281). The most recent report by the government highlighted the increase in private investment by 2.7 per cent in certain sectors, including the auto industry, due to the depreciation of the yen. However, the cost of imports rose due to the yen's depreciation and thus dampened the appetite for consumption (Oouchi and Ikuta 2015).

To summarise, in order to exit deflation and regain economic growth, PM Abe introduced Keynesian monetary coordination in order to stimulate inflation expectations, spending and therefore growth. However, as we have seen, changing market expectations has proven difficult, witnessing a failure to achieve inflation, only limited wage increases and a decrease of wages for non-regular workers, all of which has resulted in a continuation of under-consumption.

Flexible fiscal policy (the second arrow)

The so-called 'second arrow' of Abenomics has been termed 'flexible fiscal policy', and includes two large-scale fiscal packages (OECD 2015a, p. 10, Arslanap and Lam 2013). The second arrow has aimed to increase effective demand in order to end deflation and realise a virtuous cycle for the long term by increasing government expenditure (via fiscal policy) (Cabinet Office 2014b, Kataoka 2014, p. 32). This is expected to increase demand for labour, thereby reducing the number of unemployed, enabling workers to choose better jobs and hence stimulating firms to increase wages for their employees in order to attract workers (Kataoka 2014, p. 32).

The Abe administration proposed an increase in spending of 2 per cent of GDP in its supplementary budget in 2013, although this actually turned out to be much smaller (1 per cent of GDP) (Kitaoka 2013, pp. 3–4, Hausman and Wieland 2014, pp. 2–3). In the mid-term, however, Abe's fiscal policy has sought to achieve a move towards consolidation, particularly to correct fiscal conditions, which have worsened from 2007 onwards and increased to 226 per cent of GDP in 2014 (OECD 2015a, p. 31) (Arslanalp and Lam 2013, p. 23). This high volume of debt has been mitigated by Japan's low interest rates over the last two to three decades due to the large amount of purchases of JGBs by the Bank of Japan, although this low interest rate is not sustainable over the long-term as it renders Japan vulnerable to increases in interest rates (OECD 2015a, pp. 31–32). In 2013, the Abe-led government presented its fiscal strategy to halve the primary deficit of central and local governments, from 6.6 per cent of GDP in FY 2010 to 3.3 per cent by FY 2015, and to achieve a surplus by FY 2020 (OECD 2015a, p. 32). However, we have not witnessed much progress in these goals, rather seeing a worsening of public finances, particularly after the Great East Japan Earthquake in 2011, which required the government to spend about 5 per cent of GDP, including a 10.3 trillion yen (2.2 per cent of GDP) fiscal package in 2013, as well as a 5.5 trillion yen package in 2014 (OECD 2015a, pp. 32–33). The second arrow of Abenomics therefore stands on shaky ground in the sense that any fiscal stimulus has a finite limit created by the longer-term need to tackle the fiscal deficit and large amount of public debt.

As part of its attempt to improve the public finances, the Abe-led government increased consumption tax from 5 to 8 per cent in April 2014. This increase was to be spent on childcare, pensions, healthcare and social insurance (OECD 2015a, p. 33). However, this tax hike was not appreciated by Japanese consumers, prompting negative economic growth due to stagnating consumption (Harding 2015c). This negative impact of the tax hike upon the Japanese economy was criticised by many observers who argued for the importance of inflation or a stronger economic recovery before undertaking actions to achieve fiscal consolidation (Kataoka 2014, Takahashi 2014, Krugman cited in Harding 2015c). In spite of these criticisms, some economists (Hausman and Wieland 2014) emphasised the importance of Abenomics and viewed it as the right policy. However, within the Abe administration, there seems to be a divide between two camps: one camp, particularly in the Ministry of Finance, prefers spending cuts; whereas the other camp, in the Cabinet Office, has determined to prioritise economic growth over fiscal consolidation (Harding 2015a). The goal of fiscal balance has therefore been hampered by internal divisions within the Abe-led government, as well as due to the dilemma created by the sense that the increase of consumption tax is both unavoidable but also likely to dampen the effect of fiscal policy and consumer spending.

Flexible fiscal policy has also more recently turned into tightened fiscal policy due to the tax hike and the end of the fiscal stimulus packages (Harding and Inagaki 2015b). The tax hike was arguably introduced too early and put the Japanese economy back into recession in spring 2014, as households were reluctant to increase spending as prices rose as a result of the tax increase. In sum, the second arrow of Abenomics has been faced with contradictory pressures created by the need to increase public spending to stimulate the stagnating economy, at the same time as needing to limit spending due to adverse fiscal conditions. This dilemma has perhaps been most evident in the debate surrounding the recent planned increase in consumption tax.

Growth strategy (the third arrow)

The third arrow is a growth strategy, consisting of structural reforms, whereby the government pledges that it will seek to strengthen the competitiveness of domestic firms, overcome energy constraints, and enhance the innovation platform (Hausman 2014, p. 3, Yoshino and Taghizadeh-Hesary 2015, p. 8). The third arrow of structural reforms is also viewed by the Government as the most important for the success of Abenomics and Japan's long-term economic growth (Schiff 2015, p. 25, Szekeres 2015, p. 400). In setting out these reforms the Abe administration outlines ten key reforms, which include its aim to promote businesses by reducing corporate tax, improving corporate governance, encouraging venture capital and stimulating innovation through technology (Cabinet Office 2015e). These reforms also seek to reinvigorate the Japanese labour market by promoting women's participation, further flexibilising working practices, and attracting high-skilled foreign workers. Reforms further seek to enhance the liberalisation of the agricultural industry by emphasising the necessity of the participation in the Trans Pacific Partnership (TPP). The third arrow also seeks to create an environment for new growth sectors including energy, environment and health care services and its integration with Asia (Danninger and Steinberg 2015, p. 188). With these ten key reforms, the growth strategy aims to a create a 'ripple effect' across the nation and achieve two further goals: local revitalisation and the innovation of small and medium-sized enterprises (SMEs), and structural reforms in regional economies (Cabinet Office 2014a). Some of the measures set out in this strategy aim to benefit the Japanese economy. For instance, promotion of innovation and R&D in the workplace has been viewed as important for Japanese firms as well as employees. In fact, some Japanese automakers are increasing investment in new fields such as fuel-cell vehicles, with research and development expenditures reaching a record high (approximately JPY 2.5 trillion planned for FY2014) (Cabinet Office, 2015a).

However, there remain some concerns over these strategies, particularly with regard to the effectiveness of corporate tax and the further flexibilisation of the labour market. The first strategy of enhancing corporate governance is aimed at shifting Japanese corporate governance towards an Anglo-Saxon model by encouraging firms to accommodate more outside directors (Cabinet Office 2015e). This is aimed at weakening networks, including *keiretsu*, between Japanese firms. The Abe-government also aims to reduce corporate tax, which has already been reduced by 2.4 per cent since April 2014, with a target to reduce it to below 30 per cent in 2016 (Cabinet Office 2015a, p. 2, 2015b). However, the reduction of corporate tax was conducted in the 1990s, contributing in part to the deterioration of Japan's public finance (Ito 2014, p. 84). Moreover, the most profitable American firms were at that time subjected to a high corporate tax rate (40%), suggesting that the reduction of corporate tax does not necessarily guarantee the improvement of Japanese firms' productivity (Dourille-Feer 2015, p. 24).

Perhaps the most problematic aspect of the 'third arrow', however, is the goal of 'flexible working practices'. Regardless of the increasing level of poverty in Japan, which ranks sixth out of thirty-five developed countries in terms of relative income poverty (OECD 2015b), rather than focusing on measures to prevent precarious forms of employment, the initiatives chosen by the Abe administration have acted to create a further flexibilisation of working practices. PM Abe, somewhat paradoxically, directly appealed to firms to increase the wages of employees whilst at the same time implementing measures that would ensure the flexibilisation of the labour market. PM Abe's appeal will not directly increase wages but the enhancement of flexibilisation of working hours will lead to the reduction of payment for overtime and/or long-working hours without any monitoring mechanism. For instance, in terms of working hours, the structural reforms being pursued aim to 'enable flexible working practices', and improve the 'talent pool', representing an initiative to develop a more creative working practice where performance is evaluated rather than the number of working hours (Cabinet Office 2014b, p. 44). To concretely implement this initiative, there is a proposal to reform the Discretionary Working System, which allows 'creative work habits and more people to have flexible working practices' (Cabinet Office 2014b, p. 44). However, PM Abe had to withdraw this proposal due to strong criticism within the LDP, from the opposition parties and from labour, highlighting the inhibiting effect of popular discontent upon the scope for labour market reforms.

In a nutshell, what we have been witnessing as a result of flexible labour market reforms is the weakening of some of the working practices that were central to the 'classic' Japanese model, including the seniority wage system and stable employment system, and the transformation of those practices toward more performance-based and more competitive employment practices. This consolidates trends in policymaking that were already begun in the 1990s. This move towards flexibilisation is heralded by Abe himself, in that he boasts of his achievement of 'fundamental policy change from excessive employment stability to labour fluidity' (Cabinet Office 2015a, p. 3). The third arrow of Abenomics thus aims to deregulate and liberalise the labour market.

In addition to the reforms detailed above, the government also implemented reforms to the way in which new information about jobs is announced by the public employment bureau (Hello Work) to temp agencies. Some unionists, such as the chairman of *Zenroren* (the second largest trade union confederation in Japan), have argued that this reform would increase the range of job opportunities available in temp agencies, continuing to provide precarious forms of employment, and leading to increased profits for temp agencies but not for workers (Zenroren 2015). Despite the heightening criticisms of precarious employment held by non-regular workers (these criticisms were particular demonstrated in the event of *Hakenmura* (Temporary Camp for the unemployed and non-regular workers)) in December 2008, the Abe administration appears to be further accelerating the liberalisation and flexibilisation of the labour market, to the overall benefit of capital.

Furthermore, as part of the structural reforms, the Abe administration set a target to establish an improved 'labour dispute resolution system' by the end of 2015 (Cabinet Office 2014b, p. 46). This target has been set up in order to make Japanese employment practices more transparent, especially for foreign countries. The government is seeking to 'clarify ... the relationship between the amount of money paid to resolve disputes and various factors' (Cabinet Office 2014b, p. 46). Regarding this, the deregulation committee (*Kisei Kaikaku Kaigi*) started to suggest payment for mediation, labour tribunal decisions, and conciliation. This proposal has raised concerns amongst unions since it has the potential to weaken the effect of Japan's employment practices, which generally require four conditions that firms had to meet to conduct dismissal of their employees (*Syutoken Nakama Union* 2015). These four conditions imposed upon employers have in the past contributed to the low level of unemployment in the Japanese labour market. However, it is also clearly an intention of the Abe administration to lower this standard of employment regulation in Japan and shift the labour market toward a highly flexible market, whereby employers will be allowed to dismiss workers more freely as long as they pay certain costs for mediation and labour tribunal decisions.

PM Abe's attempts to encourage firms to increase wages is motivated in part by the desire to create a level of consensus between employers and employees. The new growth strategy therefore appears to include some policies that favour companies (e.g. the reduction of corporate tax and a regulation that allows more flexible working hours), but also seeks to ensure that the less competitive industries (including the agricultural sector and small- and medium-sized firms) and local economies do not lose out too much. However, the increase in consumption tax and the decrease of corporate tax tend to favour the interests of capital, to the cost of workers. Reforms suggested in the agricultural sector have also been broadly similar to the preceding DPJ government's 'new growth strategy' in the way that both strategies seek to develop the competitiveness of the agricultural sector. The Cabinet Office of Japan reports the achievement of Abenomics, including wage increases and more female workers' participation in the labour market (Cabinet Office June 2015a). However, the increase in flexible working hours, the decrease of wages of non-regular workers, and the absence of measures to reduce the number of non-regular workers, each contribute to what appears to be a longer term attempt to ensure a destabilisation of the position of workers within the Japanese labour market. These policies represent a further acceleration of neoliberalism, which, as noted above, began during the 1990s in Japan under the Hashimoto administration (1995–1998) and Koizumi administration (2001–2006) (Shibata 2016). These policies have the potential to further weaken labour's position and dampen the potentially positive effects of Abenomics. Moreover, Abenomics largely fails to benefit small- and medium-sized enterprises (SMEs) due to 'higher energy costs and other intermediate imported goods costs caused by depreciation of the yen' (Aoyagi and Ganelli 2015, p. 225) which represents an additional threat to the Japanese economy since SMEs account for 70 per cent of employees in Japan (Aoyagi and Ganelli 2015, p. 225).

Japan's GDP data suggests that its economy is struggling under Abenomics. Japan's economy grew at an annualised pace of 2.4 per cent in the first quarter of 2015 and the stock market surged with a growth in GDP forecast of 1.5 per cent. However, these increases were said to be due to a large-scale build-up in inventories. Adjusting for these factors, the actual economic growth was only 0.4 per cent (Harding 2015b). Furthermore, the Japanese economy only witnessed a moderate recovery in consumer and business spending despite the fact that the Abe-administration and the BOJ implemented a significant level of economic stimulus. Consumer spending remains stagnant due largely to the increased sales tax. Further, more than 38 per cent of the workforce are employed as non-regular workers, and thus without increases to their wages, undermining any attempt to stimulate consumption.

In sum, whilst the Keynesian remedies of the first and second arrows of Abenomics (monetary and fiscal policies) had a limited impact upon growth. Liberalisation, encouraged by the third arrow, has further destabilised the labour market, resulting in a situation whereby the effects of the growth-focused elements of the three arrows that form Abenomics are constrained further still.

Abenomics, coordination and liberalisation: an alternative growth model or repackaging old policies?

This section seeks to examine the extent to which Abenomics can be considered a coherent and alternative economic growth model, or whether it represents merely a repackaging of old policies. The article argues that Abenomics is a mix of coordination and liberalisation, as was the case in with earlier attempts to reform the Japanese economy, including those undertaken by the Koizumi (2001–2006), Hatoyama (2009–2010), Kan (2010–2011), and Noda (2011–2012) administrations, but in this instance with much stronger emphasis placed upon the liberalisation and deregulation of the Japanese economy. The article further argues that the mere repackaging of old policies will not result in improved prospects for economic growth, but rather will increase discontent, especially amongst precarious workers, which itself represents an impediment to growth.

Existing analyses of Abenomics can be roughly divided into three groups. The first group, which consists of both scholars and some of the key international organisations, broadly agree that the bundle of policies that constitute Abenomics is likely to improve Japanese economic growth, but also suggest a number of reforms to the policies, each of which seeks to further extend the degree to which the emphasis is on liberalisation of the economy. For instance, Fukao (2013) encourages the government to liberalise the Japanese market by further establishing free trade agreements and reducing corporate taxes (Fukao 2013, p. 209). Katz (2014) emphasises the importance of improving workers productivity, especially due to Japan having an aging society. He suggests that Japan needs serious structural changes, including the replacement of decaying firms with vibrant ones, and an increase in competitiveness for domestically oriented firms (which are protected from international competition by regulations) (Katz 2014). He also advocates the liberalisation of the Japanese market through the Trans-Pacific Partnership (TPP) and inducing more competition amongst industries such as the dairy market and agriculture. He further criticises the rigidities in the Japanese labour market, emphasising the importance of competition and flexibility in the workplace (2014). Similarly, the OECD urges PM Abe to implement liberalisation urgently (OECD 2015a). Three points in particular are recommended by the OECD (OECD 2015a): (1) slow the trend of decline in the labour force; (2) participate in high-level trade agreements (TPP, Japan–EU Economic Partnership Agreement); and (3) improve the business climate to boost productivity growth (liberalisation of corporate governance, promotion of labour market flexibility, reduction of corporate tax, shift towards a more market-based agricultural system). These recommendations each seek to promote the further liberalisation of the Japanese economy by prioritising the establishment of a business-friendly environment and integrating the Japanese market more deeply within the international market. In sum, for this group of scholars and international organisations, Abenomics is a step in the right direction but could be further improved through greater implementation of liberalising measures.

A second group of commentators is also broadly supportive of Abenomics, but for different reasons. This group, which includes scholars such as Krugman (2013) and Yoshino and Taghizadeh-Hesary (2014), views Abenomics positively on the grounds that it seeks to stimulate demand, inflation (over a sufficiently lengthy period of time) and restore fiscal balance (Yoshino and Taghizadeh-Hesary 2014, p. 24). Regarding the 'third arrow' of Abenomics, this second group welcomes some of the more pro-growth/pro-demand and more interventionist measures, such as the expansion of domestic consumption, attempts to encourage female participation in the labour market, measures to reduce healthcare costs to cope with the aging population, an increase in the share of R&D and education in government expenditure, and improved access to finance for SMEs (Yoshino and Taghizadeh-Hesary 2014). Paul Krugman, for instance, praises Abenomics on the grounds that it improved public expectations, Japan's fiscal outlook and the expectations of Japan's exporters (Krugman 2013). He further claims that PM Abe is making a clear break from a bad orthodoxy and that something remarkable may happen in Japan if the policies of Abenomics succeed (Krugman 2013). This second group is also, therefore, broadly supportive of Abenomics on the grounds that it represents a break with the pro-austerity and pro-liberalisation consensus that has been adopted by most of the political elite across the advanced industrial democracies. As such, Abenomics is viewed positively precisely because it is as unorthodox and unconventional.

There are, therefore, two contrasting views amongst supporters of Abenomics. On the one hand, we see those who are positive about Abenomics on the grounds that it seeks to promote consumption, investment and growth. On the other hand, there are those who believe Abenomics will be successful, provided that it includes a strong commitment to the furthering the liberalisation of Japan. What each of these interpretations misses, however, is that the liberalising elements of Abenomics also act to create insecurity for Japanese workers, whilst at the same time relying upon an expectation that there will be increased consumption – presumably from the very same workers who are experiencing heightened income insecurity. In the absence of sufficient provisions to improve the economic security of Japan's workers/consumers, therefore, it is difficult to see how a renewed social compromise (required to underpin a return to growth) can be constructed. Indeed, such a social compromise would include a set of policies and socio-economic institutions that have the potential to contain social tension and popular discontent (especially that of Japan's growing share of non-regular workers) and generate temporary economic growth. Long-term economic growth cannot be realised without both carrying out wide-ranging reforms (Patrick 2016, p. 8) and addressing declining wages and growing precarity. Non-regular workers, in particular, are vulnerable to declining income and (given that they are a growing proportion of the workforce) therefore represent a significant obstacle to attempts to stimulate consumption. In this sense, Abenomics lacks a plan through which to create a much-needed socio-economic compromise that could re-introduce some of the mechanisms of cooperation that underpinned the preceding (more successful) 'classic' model of Japanese capitalism. Without re-establishing such a compromise, moreover, firms will continue to be under pressure to reduce costs in order to be able to compete within increasingly globalising markets; weaker firms (especially SMEs) and industries (especially the agricultural industry), in particular, will be likely to become unsustainable under a heightening level of competition. As we can see, therefore, policies implemented as part of Abenomics contain a number of contradictions that might not have been fully addressed.

In addition to these underlying contradictions, Abenomics also represents (to an extent that has often gone unnoticed) a continuation of policies that have already been adopted by preceding governments, but which have thus far failed to achieve a return to growth within the Japanese economy. On these grounds, therefore, we might be less optimistic that Abenomics is able to restore growth to Japan. In particular, the third arrow of structural reforms in Abenomics shares similarities with policies implemented by the preceding governments of Nakasone, Hashimoto and Koizumi. For instance, former PM Nakasone (1982–1987) sought to increase the internationalisation of the Japanese economy, including through trade liberalisation (including that of agricultural trade), alongside attempts to achieve a flexibilisation of labour markets, and deregulation of finance (Tiberghien 2014, p. 38). The Nakasone government also sought to encourage wage rises in much the same way as PM Abe has done. The Nakasone government also similarly sought a mix of Keynesian budgetary policies and neoliberal structural reforms. There also exists a strong continuity between the reforms of Nakasone and those of the later Hashimoto administration (1996–1998), which sought to promote corporate restructuring, and deregulation and liberalisation of the financial market (Tiberghien 2014, pp. 41–42). Hashimoto's reforms intended to increase the competitiveness of Japanese firms and also enhance capital movements, thereby seeking to further integrate the Japanese economy within international markets. As such, the economic reforms of the Hashimoto administration are strikingly similar to many of those that form the ten key policies making up Abe's structural reforms.

The structural reforms that make up the 'third arrow' of Abenomics also consist of changes to existing patterns of corporate governance; aiming to relax regulations and create a business-friendly environment, including through the weakening of *keiretsu* networks so that foreign firms can be integrated in the market (OECD 2015a). In doing so, the third arrow seeks to create a more open market where foreign firms can do their business and investment more flexibly. By loosening the close *keiretsu* networks and allowing foreign firms to come into the Japanese market, the third arrow further seeks to stimulate Japanese business and make firms more internationally competitive. Again, these initiatives are not new, in that similar goals have been sought by the administrations of Nakasone,

Hashimoto and Koizumi, each of whom sought to create a more business-friendly environment by liberalising the Japanese market, reducing barriers to entry to the market for foreign actors, and lowering corporate tax for domestic and foreign firms. We can also see clear similarities between the structural reforms contained within Abenomics and those specified in the *New Growth Strategy* 2009, of the DPJ's Hatoyama administration, which included plans to achieve structural reforms in agricultural, IT and human capital, as well as seeking a regeneration of regional economies. That said, one of the key differences between Abenomics and the DPJ's strategy is the focus within Abenomics upon a much more explicit target of liberalisation and deregulation of the market in order to create a business-friendly environment and a more flexible labour market. Abenomics is, therefore, in this sense a re-packaging of old policies, but with a stronger emphasis and focus on liberalisation.

Two problems in particular arise for Abenomics as a result of its somewhat contradictory embrace of liberalisation. First, there exists an inability to produce a renewed social and institutional compromise that would enable the Abe administration to achieve coordinated improvements to Japan's political economy. For instance, in 2014, the government, *Keidanren* (the Japan Business Federation), the Japan Chamber of Commerce and Industry, the National Federation of Small Associations, and *Rengo* (the Japanese Trade Union Confederation) reached an agreement to work in cooperation regarding wage increases, wage negotiations and enhancement of productivity and improvement of treatment of non-regular workers (Rengo 2015, p. 16). This initiative, however, has faced considerable obstacles, largely due to the absence of a broader social consensus. In particular, the government has not made sufficient effort to negotiate or build a consensus with the broader network of trade unions that extends beyond the *Rengo*. This is most clearly shown by the fact that *Rengo* remains the only union confederation to be included in the negotiations on employment protection in deliberation councils attached to the Ministry of Health, Labor and Wealth (*shingikai*) (Yun 2016, p. 475). Indeed, a number of criticisms of the government by other union confederations, including that it has failed to sufficiently include other unions and union confederations, have been made. The Abe government has not included non-*Rengo* unions in its decision-making process, with the absence of unions representing non-regular workers being particularly notable (Ministry of Health, Labour and Weath, 2016).[1] One noteworthy consequence of this has been the failure of the Abe administration to achieve its stated goal of encouraging firms to raise wages. Abenomics therefore appears to be faltering, both in terms of its efforts to introduce a greater degree of socio-economic coordination and to achieve a greater degree of compromise between different trade unions and different types of workers.

Second, the shift in resources that is taking place from wages to profits, has had a detrimental effect upon consumption and saving patterns. Ito (2014) warns that the Abe government seeks a labour market in which companies are much more free to hire and fire at will, can employ non-regular workers with cheap wages, and have no legal obligation to pay overtime (Ito 2014, pp. 62–63). In a similarly critical tone, FT columnist Martin Wolf expressed his concerns over 'excessive private savings' and reported that excessive retained earnings should be lowered via increasing wages and changing corporate taxation (Wolf 2013). Similarly, Yamada and Hirano (2015) highlight the way in which management in Japanese firms has responded to shareholder pressure by providing greater dividends and increasing its own internal reserves, without distributing wealth to workers. From this perspective, the third arrow fails to sufficiently incorporate a broader segment of the economy, that is, its workers. This both acts to deepen discontent amongst workers (who suffer from employment insecurity and stagnating wages) but also (relatedly) acts to contribute to under-consumption. Clearly this is a problem for Abenomics in that one of its central aims is to create a virtuous circle in which we see a mutually reinforcing increase in investment, income and consumption.

Indeed, one of the central problems facing Japan's economy is that Japanese firms have retained and accumulated a high level of cash, which has acted to restrain aggregate demand and potential output growth (Shinada 2012, cited in OECD 2015a, p. 24). Throughout the 2000s, the proportion of cash holdings in the Japanese corporate sector has been much higher than in the corporate sectors in the US and European Union (OECD 2015a, p. 25). This problem could be solved by increasing wages (to stimulate consumption) and/or increasing investment. The net return on capital in Japan has been increasing since the introduction of Abenomics (Roberts 2015), but appeals by the Abe-led government, calling on firms to increase wages for their employees, have not so far been heeded within the business circle, resulting in the continuation of stagnating wage growth in Japan. This perhaps illustrates the limited means by which firms can be persuaded to limit profit-seeking and increase wages (Harding and Inagaki 2015b).

The alternative growth model requires socio-economic institutions that coordinate different interests and can contain discontent among workers and improve precarious workers' conditions. However, Japanese firms do not appear to share their retained earnings through an increase of wages or labour protection. As a result, the government has been further pressured to implement a negative interest rates policy and further quantitative easing. Without addressing contentious issues surrounding workers, and establishing coordination and compromise between capital and labour, Abenomics (which is built upon on liberalisation in a similar way to other political reforms conducted by political elites, including former prime ministers, Hashimoto and Koizumi) faces obstacles to both its implementation and successful execution. PM Abe's recent decision to further postpone his second planned consumption tax rise until October 2019 (another two-year postponement) reflects the fact that Abenomics has not thus far resulted in a stable economic growth model. Indeed, if Abenomics cannot produce a stable alternative growth model, able to coordinate capital–labour relations by improving employment conditions, achieving more equity between regular and non-regular workers and employment security, including labour in decision-making processes and increasing labour's share of income, it is likely instead to lead to a further increase in the level of discontent, especially on the part of its increasingly insecure labour force. Heightening discontent amongst workers in this sense represents an obstacle to the smooth implementation of Abenomics and in turn undermines the ability to improve the Japanese economy.

Conclusion

This article examines the existing literature on Abenomics and present a preliminary analysis of the overall aims and outcomes of Abenomics in order to explore the extent to which Abenomics has contributed to the growth or non-growth of Japan's economy. It questions the extent to which Abenomics represents an alternative growth model for the Japanese economy, and highlights the key challenges that Abenomics faces. Whilst some commentators (including Krugman, Posen and Hausman) have tended to highlight the strength of Abenomics on the grounds that it represents an unconventional demand-oriented alternative to the pro-austerity and pro-liberalisation consensus, a second group of commentators and international institutions broadly agree with the liberalising measures that also constitute Abenomics (whilst also pointing to the importance of further strengthening these liberalising measures) (Fukao 2013, Katz 2014, OECD 2015a). Finally, a third group of commentators – with which this paper is most sympathetic – have raised concerns about Abe's structural reforms, on the grounds that they have the potential to destabilise the labour market (Ito 2014, Wolf 2014, Roberts 2015, Yamada and Hirano 2015).

Partly agreeing with the critique made by this third group of commentators, this article argues that Abenomics represents a mix of Keynesian remedies in the financial and monetary policies and neoliberal policies in terms of structural reforms. However, in seeking to both stimulate demand and introduce structural reforms, the potential positive effects of both strategies are limited as a result of their mutual incompatibility. Wage growth has been contained and working conditions surrounding precarious workers remain unstable, leading to stagnating consumption and hence investment. Thus, the attempt to stimulate demand through so-called 'flexible fiscal policy' has been undermined by attempts under the so-called 'third arrow' to create more flexible markets (and especially labour markets), as the latter set of policies have introduced a greater degree of economic insecurity (especially for Japanese workers). Further, Abenomics has been shown to be less different from the policies of previous Japanese administrations than is often assumed. In this sense, Abenomics represents a repackaging of policies, albeit with a stronger emphasis upon liberalisation. Finally, the article shares the concerns expressed by a third group of commentators who point to the limited effect that Abenomics is likely to have upon the economy, in particular due to its continued commitment to an unfair and unequal distribution of wealth, to the detriment of Japan's workers, which, in the past, has undermined attempts to achieve a coordinated intervention in Japan's political economy (Ito 2014, Wolf 2014, Roberts 2015, Yamada and Hirano 2015).

Rather than being an alternative growth model, therefore, Abe's neoliberal policy package poses a threat to the stability of Japan's economy. Despite the apparently positive initial impact that Abenomics has had upon stock prices, the reduction of the unemployment rate and the small increase in wages, the 'third arrow' has witnessed an attempt to deregulate Japan's labour market, and in the process imposed a greater burden on labour, and especially the growing number of non-regular workers who have been losing protection and suffering increased precarity in terms of wages and employment status within Japan's changing political economy. Any wage increases that have occurred in recent years have been secured through bonuses or overtime work payments, rather than changes to the standard salary (Ministry of Economy, Trade and Industry 2014), thereby evincing the reluctance of corporations to share any increases in national income or wealth. Workers (and especially non-regular workers) have suffered from stagnating wages, and growing income insecurity as a result of the flexibilisation of labour. Currently, more than 38 per cent of Japan's workforce is employed as non-regular workers. Without the reintroduction of some form of socio-economic compromise, through which this group of workers can be more equitably incorporated into the Japanese economic model, it is difficult to see how Abenomics will be able to generate economic growth in the long term. Those Keynesian-style remedies that are part of Abenomics have not been able to address Japan's longer-term problem of weak demand, especially of the lack of private consumption. Whilst Abenomics has the potential (at least in the short-to-medium term) to improve the profitability of Japanese business, therefore, without witnessing a corresponding move to redistribute wealth to labour, Abenomics represents a hazard to the future economic growth of Japan.

Acknowledgements

I am grateful for helpful comments from Sébastien Lechevalier, David Chiavacci and the anonymous reviewers.

Disclosure statement

No potential conflict of interest was reported by the author.

Note

1. Members of councils (Shingikai meibo)

References

Aoyagi, C. and Ganeli, G., 2015. 'Labor Market Reform: Vital to the Success of Abenomics', In: Botman, D.P.J, et al., 2015. *Can Abenomics succeed?: Overcoming the legacy of Japan's lost decades*. IMF.

Arslanap, S and Lam, R.W., 2013. 'Outlook for Interest Rates and Japanese Banks: Risk Exposures under Abenomics', *IM Working Papers*, 13/213. Available from: https://www.imf.org/external/pubs/cat/longres.aspx?sk=40994.0 [Accessed January 2016].

Boyer, R., Uemura, H., and Isogai, A., 2012. *Diversity and Transformation of East Asian Capitalism*. London: Routledge.

Cabinet Office, 2014a. 'Immediate Economic Measures for Extended Virtuous Cycles to Local Economies', December 27, 2014. Available from: http://www5.cao.go.jp/keizai1/keizaitaisaku/2014/141227_economic_measures_all.pdf [Accessed 4 September 2015].

Cabinet Office, 2014b. *Japan Revitalization Strategy: Revised in 2014 – Japan's challenge for the future-*, Cabinet Office June 24, 2014. Available from: http://www.kantei.go.jp/jp/singi/keizaisaisei/pdf/honbunEN.pdf [Accessed 4 September 2015].

Cabinet Office, 2015a. *"Japan Revitalization Strategy": Main Achievements to Date and Further Reforms*, March 2015. Available from: http://www.kantei.go.jp/jp/singi/keizaisaisei/pdf/seika02shousaiEN.pdf [Accessed 4 September 2015].

Cabinet Office, 2015b. 'Achievements of the "third arrow" reforms and new measure to be taken', March 2015. Available from: http://www.kantei.go.jp/jp/singi/keizaisaisei/pdf/seika01gaiyouEN.pdf [Accessed 4 September 2015].

Cabinet Office, 2015c. Abenomics: Decisive Action of Reform ~There is no alternative~ [Abenomikusu: Kaikaku no Dankou ~Kono Michi shika Nai]. June 2015. Available from: http://www.kantei.go.jp/jp/singi/keizaisaisei/pdf/kaikakudankouJP.pdf [Accessed 4 September 2015].

Cabinet Office, 2015d. Business Statistics, Consumer Confidence Index,Consumer Perception Indices. Available from:http://www.esri.cao.go.jp/en/stat/shouhi/shouhi-e.html#cci [Accessed 4 September 2015].

Cabinet Office, 2015e. Revision of Japan Revitalization Strategy ~ 10 Key Reforms. Available from: http://www.kantei.go.jp/jp/singi/keizaisaisei/pdf/10challenge02shousaiEN.pdf [Accessed 4 September 2015].

Danninger, S. and Steinberg, C., 2015. Japan's growth challenge: needs and potential. In: Botman, D.P.J, et al., 2015. *Can Abenomics succeed?: overcoming the legacy of Japan's lost decades*. IMF.

Dourille-Feer, E., 2015. 'Can the Magic of Abenomics Succeed?', *CEPIIWorking Paper*. Available from: http://www.cepii.fr/PDF_PUB/wp/2015/wp2015-24.pdf [Accessed April 2016].

Estévez-Abe, M., 2008. *Welfare and Capitalism in Postwar Japan*. New York: Cambridge University Press.

Fujiwara, I., Nakazono, Y., Ueda, K., 2014. 'Policy Regime Change against Chronic Deflation? Policy option under long-term liquidity trap', *AJRC Working Paper*, April 2014, Available from: https://papers.ssrn.com/sol3/papers.cfm?abstract_id=2446759 [Accessed January 2017].

Fukao, K., 2013. 'Explaining Japan's Unproductive Two Decades', Asian Economic Policy Review, 8, pp. 193–213.

Fukuda, S., 2015. 'Abenomics: Why was it so successful in changing market expectations?', *CIRJE Discussion Papers*, CIRJE-F-969.

Hall, P.A. and Soskice, D., 2001. 'An introduction to Varieties of Capitalism', in P.A. Hall and D. Soskice (eds), Varieties of Capitalism: The Institutional Foundations of Comparative Advantage, Oxford: Oxford University Press.

Harding, R. and Inagaki, K., 2015b. Japan wages: Manufacturing consent. *Financial Times*, 18 February.

Harding, R., 2015a. 'Japan experts defend Abenomics go for growth' strategy', Financial Times, May 24, 2015.

Harding, R., 2015b. 'Japan GDP data suggest struggle for a momentum', *Financial Times*, 20 May.

Harding, R. 2015c. 'World watches Japan and waits for outcome of Abenomics experiments', *Financial Times*, 29 March.

Harding, R. and Inagaki, K., 2015a. 'Japan wages: Manufacturing consent', in Financial Times, February 18, 2015.

Hausman, J.K. and Wieland, J. F., 2014. 'Abenomics: Preliminary Analysis and Outlook' Brookings Paper, Spring 2014, pp. 1–63.

Imai, J., 2011. *Transformation of Japanese Employment Relations: Reform without Labour*. Basingstoke: Palgrave Macmillan.

IMF, 2013. "Japan: 2013 Article IV Consultation," IMF Country Report No. 13/253, August 5, 2013.

Isogai, A., 2012. 'The transformation of the Japanese corporate system and the hierarchical nexus of institutions', in Boyer et al. (eds.), Diversity and Transformation of Asian Capitalism. London: Routledge.

Ito, M., 2014. *Critique of Abenomics: Break Four Arrows* [Abenomics Hihan: Yon Hon no Ya wo Oru]. Tokyo: Iwanami Syoten.

Jeong, D.Y. and Aguilera, R.V., 2008. 'The Evolution of Enterprise Unionism in Japan: Socio-Political Perspective', *British Journal of Industrial Relations*, 46 (1), 98–132.

Kataoka, G., 2014. Why hasn't Japan's economy recovered yet? [Naze Nihonkeizai ha Fujyo Shinainoka]. Tokyo: Koubunsyashinsyo.

Katz, R., 2014. 'Voodoo Abenomics: Japan's failed comeback plan', *Foreign Affairs*, 93 (4), 133–141.

Kitaoka, S., 2013. 'The Abe Administation: Beyond 100 Days', *Asia-Pacific Review*, 20 (1), 1–12.

Krugman, P., 2013. 'Japan Steps Out', New York Times, January 13, 2013.

Krugman, P., 2014. 'Japan Through the Looking Glass', New York Times, November 16, 2014.

Lechevalier, S., 2014. Introduction: Seven Japanese lessons on the diversity of capitalism and its future. *In:* S. Lechevalier, ed. *The great transformation of Japanese capitalism*. Oxon: Routledge.

Ministry of Economy, Trade and Industry, 2014, 'Chinage Jyoukyou nitsuite', September 2014. Available from: http://www5.cao.go.jp/keizai-shimon/kaigi/minutes/2014/0916/sankou_02.pdf [Accessed 4 September 2015].

Ministry of Health, Labour and Welfare, 2010. *White Paper on Labour and Economy 2010*. Available from: http://www.mhlw.go.jp/wp/hakusyo/kousei/10/ [Accessed 15 December 2013].

Ministry of Health, Labour and Welfare, 2010. *White Paper on Labour and Economy 2010*. Available from http://www.mhlw.go.jp/wp/hakusyo/kousei/10/ [Accessed 15 December 2013].

Ministry of Health, Labour and Welfare, 2015. *Maitsuki Kinrou Toukei Chousa, Gekkan Genkin Kyuyogaku*, May, 2015. Available from: http://www.mhlw.go.jp/toukei/itiran/roudou/monthly/27/2705p/2705p.html[Accessed 4 September 2015].

Ministry of Health, Labour and Welfare, 2013. *White Paper on Labour and Economy 2013*. Available from http://www.mhlw.go.jp/wp/hakusyo/roudou/13/dl/13-1-3_01.pdf [Accessed 4 September 2015].

Ministry of Health, Labour and Welfare, 2016. *A list of members of labour deliberation council* [Shingikai].

OECD, 2015a. *OECD Economic Surveys: Japan*, April 2015. Available from: http://www.keepeek.com/Digital-Asset-Management/oecd/economics/oecd-economic-surveys-japan-2015_eco_surveys-jpn-2015-en#page22 [Accessed 4 September 2015].

OECD, 2015b. Relative Income Poverty, *In*: *OECD Income Distribution Database*, 2015. Available from: http://www.oecd.org/social/income-distribution-database.htm[Accessed 4 September 2015].

Ohishi, K., 2015, Private Investment in Japanese Economy, Nagoya Gakuin Daigaku Ronsyu. *Social Science*, 51 (4), 281–289.

Oouchi and Ikuta, 2015. Enyasu tanomi, Setsubitoushi ga zouka Kozinsyouhi ha Moriagari Kaku, *Asahi Shinbun Digita*l 8 June, 2015. Available from: http://www.asahi.com/articles/ASH685CQSH68ULFA01W.html[Accessed 4 September 2015].

Patrick, H., 2016. 'Japan's Abenomics Bumps Along', *Occasional Paper Series*, no.74, Available from: www.gsb.columbia.edu/cjeb/research.

Rebick, M., 2005. *The changing Japanese employment system*. Oxford: Oxford University Press.

Rengo, 2015, *Rengo chingin report 2014*. Available from: http://www.jtuc-rengo.or.jp/roudou/shuntou/2014/shuukei_bunseki/22.html [Accessed 4 September 2015]

Roberts, M., 2014. Abenomics: raises profitability ... and misery, Michael Roberts Blog, 2014, July. Available from: https://thenextrecession.wordpress.com/2014/07/ [Accessed January 2016].

Roberts, M., 2015. 'Japan: the failure of Abenomics', Available from: https://thenextrecession.wordpress.com/2014/10/13/japan-the-failure-of-abenomics/ [Accessed May 2015]

Rosenbluth, F.M. and Thies, M.F., 2010. *Japan Transformed: Political Change and Economic Restructuring*. Woodstock: Princeton University.

Schaede, U., 2004. 'What Happened to the Japanese Model?', *Review of International Economics*, 12 (2), 277–294.

Schiff, J., 2015. Abenomics: From the Lost Decade to the Three Arrows. *In*: D.P.J. Botman, S. Danninger and J. Schiff, eds. *Can Abenomics Succeed?: Overcoming the Legacy of Japan's Lost Decades*. Washington: IMF.

Shibata, S., 2016. 'Resisting Japan's neoliberal model of capitalism: intensification and change in contemporary patterns of class struggle, *British Journal of Industrial Relations*, 54 (3), 496–521.

Szekeres, V. 2015. *Abenomics:a Way to Accelerate the Japanese Economic Growth?, Management, Enterprise and Benchmarking in the 21st Century, Budapest, 2015*. Available from: https://ideas.repec.org/h/pkk/meb015/397-404.html [Accessed May 2016].

Takahashi, Y., 2014. *Counterattack of Abenomics [Abenomics no Gyakusyu]*. Tokyo: PHP Kenkyusyo.

Tiberghien, Y., 2014. Thirty years of neoliberal reforms in Japan. *In*: S. Lechevalier, ed. *The great transformation of Japanese capitalism*. Oxon, Routledge.

Uchida, M., 2014. Towards the end of deflation in Japan?: monetary policy under Abenomics and the role of the central bank. *Revue de l'OFCE*, 135.

Ueda, K., 2013. Response of asset prices to monetary policy under Abenomics. *Asian Economic Policy Review*, no.8, 252–269.

Uemura, H. and Tahara, S., 2014. The Transformation of Growth Regime and de-industrialization in Japan. *Revue de la régulation*, 15, Spring 2014

Uemura, H., 2012. Nihon Keizai no Seidohenka to Seityo Taisei: Aratana Kouzouteki Kikie. *In*: H. Uni, et al., *Kinyu Kiki no Regurashion Riron: Nihon Keizai no Kadai*. Tokyo: Syowado.

Vogel, S.K., 2006. *Japan Remodeled: How Government and Industry Are Reforming Japanese Capitalism*. New York, NY: Cornell University Press.

Watanabe, R.H., 2012. 'Why and how did Japan finally change its ways? The politics of Japanese labour-market deregulation since the 1990s', Japan Forum, 24 (1), 23–50.

Weathers, C., 2008. Shunto and the shackles of competitiveness. *Labor History*, 49(2), 177–197.

Witt, M.A., 2006. *Changing Japanese Capitalism: Societal Coordination and Institutional Adjustment*. Cambridge: Cambridge University Press.

Wolf, M., 2013. Japan can put people before profits: The key to a better-balanced economy is to take surplus profits away from a corporate oligopoly. *Financial Times*, 5 February, 2013.

Wolf, M., 2014. Warning from Japan for the eurozone. *Financial Times*, 4 November, 2014.

Yamada, T. and Hirano, Y., 2012. 'How had the Japanese mode of regulation changed?', in Boyer, R. Uemura, H. and Isogai, A., 2012. Diversity and Transformation of East Asian Capitalism. London: Routledge.

Yamada, T. and Hirano Y., 2015. *Multinationalization of Japanese firms and dysfunction of company-ist regulation. International conference research and regulation: the theory of regulation in times of crises*, 9–12 June 10–12, 2015 Paris: Université Paris-Diderot.

Yoshino, N. and Taghizadeh-Hesary, F., 2014. Three arrows of 'Abenomics' and the structural reform of Japan: inflation targeting policy of the central bank, fiscal consolidation, and growth strategy. August 2014, No.492.

Yoshino, N. and Taghizadeh-Hesary, F., 2015. Three arrows of "Abenomics" and the structural reform of Japan: inflation targeting policy of the central bank, fiscal consolidation, and growth strategy, *ADBI Working Paper Series*, No.492, August 2014.

Yun, J., 2010. Unequal 'Japan: conservative corporatism and labour market. *British Journal of Industrial Relations*, 48(1), 1–25.

Yun, J., 2016. 'The setback in political entrepreneurship and employment dualization in Japan, 1998-2012', *British Journal of Industrial Relations*, 54 (3), 473–495.

Zenroren, 2015. Zenroren Non-Regular Workers' Center News [Zenroren/Hiseiki Center News], vol. 27. Available from: http://www.cwac.jp/blog/files/cwac_news27.pdf [Accessed January 2016].

Index